EARTHLY GOOD

EARTHLY GOOD

THE CHURCHES AND THE BETTERMENT OF HUMAN EXISTENCE

by Kenneth Hamilton

WILLIAM B. EERDMANS PUBLISHING COMPANY
GRAND RAPIDS, MICHIGAN

Library of Congress Cataloging-in-Publication Data

Hamilton, Kenneth.
  Earthly good: the churches and the betterment of human
existence / by Kenneth Hamilton.
         p.   cm.
  ISBN 0-8028-0484-5
  1. Theology—Methodology. 2. Church and the world. 3. Sociology,
Christian. 4. Church and social problems. I. Title.
BR118.H36 1990
261'.09'045—dc20   90-32754
                                                           CIP

Contents

CONTENTS

Preface

Heaven's my destination. In the 1930s Thornton Wilder adopted these words to provide a title for his novel about evangelism in the Midwest. They are words no longer heard in that region—or anywhere else. Instead, with extraordinary unanimity, Christian preachers all over the world are commending the gospel on the grounds of the good it can bring about on this earth. Whereas Christians formerly were urged to endure present ills in the hope of a better life hereafter, today they are being told to expect a better life here and now.

For the mainline or ecumenical churches, the good flowing from the Christian faith is said to be the advancement of social justice, human rights, and world peace. Among the conservative churches traditionally emphasizing individual salvation, the good is stated in terms of personal health and happiness together with the reversal of the contemporary trend toward the decline in public moral standards. In either case, the appeal is to an earthly good desired for its own sake.

Of course, Christians have always been concerned about serving God and their neighbors in this world as well as about preparing themselves for the next one. Yet earthly good used to be judged in the light of the revelation that came from heaven, and was distinguished from the values cherished in an unbelieving world. The change that has come about is that now the churches seem to have accepted in a wholesale manner the ideas concerning what is good that are current in the society around them. Thus, the distinction between being *in* the world and being *of* the world has been either blurred or totally erased.

This is the situation addressed in the following pages. I shall try to answer three questions. First, how has it come about that so many churches in Europe and America alike have reduced the Christian message to one almost indistinguishable from what is being said in the secular world? Second, what is the nature and substance of current teaching and preaching in these churches? Third, in what ways does a gospel revised for present-day consumption conflict with the traditional gospel? The three questions are interconnected, the first two being especially closely tied together. So, in part one I shall consider mainly the first two questions. In part two I shall examine the third question, suggesting how traditional Christian beliefs can be applied to the contemporary political, social, and cultural scene. This last subject, naturally, is too complex to be covered in a single book. My suggestions in this area are merely sketches of a possible Christian critique of widely accepted views about our corporate existence. My central theme is that when Christians propose to advance earthly good, they should first be very sure in their own minds how good for created men and women is to be distinguished from evil. From the Christian perspective, much that seems good is an illusion created by our perennial temptation to follow our own inclinations rather than to seek the will of God for us.

If the majority of names quoted in the text are those of Europeans, this is because the chief influences upon twentieth-century theology—at least until very recently—have originated in Europe. But the developments I am discussing are essentially worldwide. Authors on this side of the Atlantic have taken up the theme as one fully applicable to the American churches. Donald G. Bloesch's *The Invaded Church* (1975) and Vernard Eller's *Towering Babble: God's People Without God's Word* (1983) deal cogently with the topics presented in my Part One. Eller's recent work *Christian Anarchy: Jesus' Primacy Over the Powers* (1987) treats in a highly original way many of the questions I discuss in part two. A wealth of detailed documentation is to be found in Harry Antonides's *Stones for Bread; The Social Gospel and its Contemporary Legacy* (1985), which is a study of the churches in Canada. I mention these three authors because I have benefitted greatly not only from their writings but also from personal conversations with them. But the list of books to which I am indebted for insight into my subject could go on and on.

My friend Dirck de Vos has read my manuscript in various stages of its development. I cannot thank him sufficiently for his critical advice and encouragement.

For the sake of ease in reading I have dispensed with footnotes—regretfully, because as well as giving precise pointers to the sources used footnotes allow little asides directed to the reader. Biblical references are mostly from the Revised Standard Version, although other versions have been used when their wording seemed best fitted to the context. The translations used are indicated as follows: JB—The Jerusalem Bible; KJV—King James Version; NEB—New English Bible; NIV—New International Version; RSV—Revised Standard Version.

KENNETH HAMILTON
Winnipeg, Canada

The Argument

Today the churches think they face a secular society unin-
terested in either God or heaven. In order to placate this society
they preach a salvation to come on this earth. Adopting the slogan *liberation!* they explain how the Christian gospel is a message about people working together to create a just society freed
from oppressive establishments. Yet it is by no means certain
that contemporary society is as monolithic in its secularity as the
churches believe it to be. So, while claiming to further earthly
good, the preaching and teaching of the churches result rather
in ignoring concrete good and evil as these are actually found
on earth. Abstract theories are preferred to facts.

One such theory is that society is progressing inevitably
towards the goal of a secular utopia. This theory, which was a
foundational myth of eighteenth-century Enlightenment thinkers, is clearly at odds with traditional Christian teaching on
Original Sin. The churches, therefore, downplay sin and speak
much of human potential. A second theory is that of ancient
Gnosticism, a body of religious beliefs which held the created
world to be evil and salvation to consist in freeing the human
spirit from time and space. Put together, these two widely different beliefs inspire the new version of the gospel heard so
often today. Jesus Christ becomes the symbol for the creative
potentialities of the human spirit. When these potentialities become fully liberated from the evils dominating the world until
now, the utopia of a fully humanized world will arrive. Chris-

tians, seeing God to be in other people, will help in the process of transforming the earth into a place of love seen in action.

Traditional Christian faith sees the new gospel as a message of hate rather than of love—hate for the earth God has created. The gospel is a message for every generation and not one about a coming utopia. This world can be reformed in part. It cannot be transformed until God brings in his kingdom, which will be a new heaven and a new earth. God's kingdom is now present, though, wherever believers accept the forgiving grace that came to this earth in the person of Jesus Christ. People do not need to be humanized. God has created them human beings. They need to be reborn through the action of God's Holy Spirit. Those who are in Christ do not have to be liberated, because they are already free.

For traditional Christians, heavenly and earthly good are not mutually exclusive. The Word that came down from heaven reveals the nature of earthly good and how it may be found. Wishing to create the earth over again in our own image is precisely the meaning of *sin*. When we love this earth as God's handiwork, living and working upon earth is viewed as both a duty and a joy. We do not seek to be liberated from the present but only from the evils that human sin has brought. We can seek to make human communities resemble more nearly the spheres of mutual love which God intended them to be. This is to advance earthly good. But the illusion that human effort can turn this world into a utopia is not merely productive of no earthly good. It is likely to result in creating a hell upon earth.

ONE THE RETREAT FROM THE CHRISTIAN TRADITION: PRODIGAL CHURCHES

1. A Strange Agenda

Herein lies the mission of the church: it is to participate in the movements of human liberation in our time in such a way as to witness to Jesus Christ as the Source, the Judge, and the Redeemer of the human spirituality and its orientation as it is at work in such movements, and therefore as the Saviour of Man today.

M. M. Thomas, former Chairman of the Central
Committee of the World Council of Churches

When in 1948 the World Council of Churches was founded in Amsterdam, its watchword was, "Let the Church be the Church!" Twenty years later that watchword had changed to, "Let the World write the Agenda!"

The change did not result from any declared shift in policy. Rather, it was the result of altered thinking about the meaning of the Christian faith that had permeated many churches, chiefly in Europe and America, and had brought to the fore the idea of a secular Christianity. Today the church was no longer to look inward but to justify her existence by serving a needy world and upholding human dignity.

Not only was the world to set the agenda for the church. It was also to provide the method for implementing the agenda. In *The Naked Public Square: Religion and Democracy in America* (1984), Richard John Neuhaus tells how a mainline bishop explained to him, "The mission of the church is to build the king-

3

dom of God on earth, and the means of the mission is politics."
Neuhaus notes how American church leaders seem to equate
true politics with the policies of the left wing of the Democratic
party. He writes, "Among the leadership of mainline Protestantism—not necessarily the membership—in the 1980s the
prayer was for the second coming of a George McGovern, assuming that FDR was no longer available."

My purpose in these pages is not to review the widespread
nature of the way in which selectively chosen politics has become a preoccupation of church leaders. The evidence for this
trend is visible all around us. My concern is with the development of a particular way of looking at the Christian faith giving
rise to politicized church strategies. In this connection the opinions of M. M. Thomas are very revealing. While giving a viewpoint especially reflecting the general outlook of the WCC, they
indicate presuppositions that have gained such wide currency
that they also exist in sections of evangelical Protestantism, as
well as among "liberal" thinkers in Roman Catholic circles.

For Dr. Thomas, the church is to put her entire trust in
the politics of liberation. Yet, while liberation sounds wonder-
ful in the abstract, its concrete expressions are always
questionable. No movement has ever been organized to advance human liberation per se. Instead, some special group
demands liberation for itself. The demands of different
groups are conflicting and sometimes contradictory—liberation of one group resulting in oppression of another. A liberation movement not motivated by self-interest would be impossible to find. Thus the agenda for the church proposed by
Dr. Thomas is a strange one. It is strange because it is alien to
the traditionally held mission of the church to preach the
gospel and to build up her members in the faith. And it is
strange because it lacks credibility.

This agenda is justified apparently on the grounds that
participation in liberation movements will allow church members to witness to Jesus Christ as Savior. Yet this justification is
weakened by what Dr. Thomas says a little later, when he ob-
serves,

The spiritual creativity behind today's revolutionary search for a society which harnesses nature through science and technology for human welfare, eliminates poverty and oppression, opens the door of participation in power structures to hitherto submerged groups, and moves towards a fraternity of free and equal persons has its source, in part at least, in Christ's salvation of the human spirit. One could speak of it as a new stage in God's process of creation.

Here it appears that the indirect witness of the churches can be, at the most, a witness to a Christ who is part Savior of the human spirit. Today's spiritual creativity belongs to a process dependent upon God, perhaps, but not upon God in Christ. So the church's witness to Jesus Christ cannot be unequivocal.

Dr. Thomas assumes the new stage in God's process of creation now dawning to be a self-evident fact. Yet he provides no proof that our present "revolutionary" search for a fraternity of free and equal persons has turned out any better than the age-old search of the human race for a better society. Every thinking person today knows very well that our efforts to harness nature through science and technology have been ambiguous in their results. After World War II, the discovery of DDT and the building of giant dams were considered breakthroughs that would bring the developing countries to rapid prosperity. At this date, these presumed blessings are judged to have been disastrous in their long-term effects. What applies in the scientific and technological realms applies to a far greater extent in the social, political, and economic realms. The most notable result of the rise of liberation movements, for example, has been the modern phenomenon of international terrorism—for one person's terrorist is another person's freedom fighter. Even when liberation movements eschew violence and work through democratic structures, they also have increased what one contemporary educator has called "the tyranny of sectional interests." In anything concerning human welfare, reappraisals of the suitability of means to ends are continually needed. Socialism has long been widely advocated by church leaders as superior to capitalism because it looks to the needs of society as a whole, while capitalism regards only the profit motive and therefore is selfish and unchristian. Ironically, church bodies and Catholic and Protestant bishops were still repeating this viewpoint at the time when ideologically socialist countries, including Russia and China, were reintroducing the profit motive, not simply for economic reasons but equally in order to create a sense of worth and dignity among the workers. It will be interesting to see whether the extraordinary developments in Eastern Europe will at all modify future pronouncements by church leaders on the evils of Western capitalism.

Rhetoric about a new stage in creation fills nobody's stomach and releases no political prisoner. The unanimity of so many church leaders over adopting the new agenda of social salvation is remarkable. It is a matter of some puzzlement to the rank-and-file members, who for the most part do not share the enthusiasm of their pastors and masters for an updated gospel. Social observers (whether professional sociologists, journalists, or novelists) find the situation less surprising. Chiefly, they see it as the cultural captivity of ecclesiastical institutions. Having largely lost their former roles as the spiritual and moral guardians of society, church leaders are trying to regain their place in the sun. Since in a pluralistic culture lacking long-established common traditions politics has become increasingly the means of defining social norms, church leaders turn to political action as a means of gaining attention. Whether this course will bring them social prestige is somewhat doubtful. The unchurched are likely to view it as meddling. Their own followers, holding many varieties of political views themselves, will certainly fear that the denomination they belong to is being forced into one political ideology.

The churches' changeover to a politicized stance did not happen overnight. And how it came about is important, since the *how* is always part of the *why*. The change cannot be explained entirely by pressure from the surrounding culture. There were internal causes as well as external ones. The Protestant denominations for a long time had lost confidence in their traditional credal doctrines and were ripe for a cultural invasion after years of cultural accommodation and compromise. Today's churches are the heirs of a fatal legacy.

6

This legacy is a mindset fearful of insufficient movement with the times and too much subservience to the latest fashions in contemporary thought. Numerous Protestant theologians and clergy have imagined for generations that the way to preach the gospel effectively was to make its message palatable to the modern mind. Only a minority at any one time has argued that the reverse was true: that what the churches had to offer an unbelieving world was precisely what that world did not have—the Christ of the New Testament and of the historic creeds; and that the churches' faithfulness to their foundational confessions alone could justify their continued existence. As a consequence, having sown the wind, mainline Protestant denominations are now reaping the whirlwind in the form of drastically decreasing influence, prestige, and numbers. Apparently, this outcome has not brought about any reappraisal of their strategies but rather a determination to push harder and faster along the same course.

The Roman Catholic Church, on the other hand, has not yielded to the pressures of cultural change to nearly the same extent. Fortified by her stand upon the twin foundations of Scripture and tradition, this church has never doubted the prime importance of Christian doctrine for maintaining her life and influence over society. It is often said that with the Second Vatican Council (1962-65) Rome finally entered the twentieth century. If so, it was a very tentative entry. Latin is not the language of the mass media, and the work of the Council evidenced as little concession to the spirit of modernity as did the language in which it was conducted. Yet very many Catholic theologians have argued that the *spirit* of the Council went beyond the *letter* of its documents. On this basis, they have gone on to press for a reversal of the traditional Catholic stand on such moral and social issues as contraception, abortion, divorce, the ordination of women, and clerical celibacy. Individual radical Catholics are largely indistinguishable from their Protestant counterparts. For their numbers, they are given much publicity.

Secularized culture, then, has suggested the agenda for the Protestant churches and has influenced, at least here and there, the agenda of the church of Rome. But it is not culture that has written the agenda. This has been done by leaders and teachers within the churches themselves.

The values presupposed in the agenda are secular. The methods—political action through pressure groups or, in the last resort, violent revolution—are secular. Yet the language remains stubbornly religious. And not the language alone. When church leaders invoke the names of God and Christ in connection with human liberation, this is no mere windowdressing concealing an intention to promote a secular creed. They have no desire to turn their churches into secular institutions. All the evidence suggests otherwise. For them, the strange agenda is a bold call to promote authentic Christianity in the form needed for facing the world of today and tomorrow, one demanding a living and active faith instead of an echo from a dead past.

My argument in these pages is that proponents of the strange agenda are preaching a religion, certainly, but a religion using Christian words to present a wholly pagan view of the universe. The politicized gospel they preach is not wrong because it advocates Christian involvement in society. It is wrong because it is at odds entirely with the historic Christian faith. Because its view both of the individual and of society is not Christian, it makes impossible a Christian approach to social, political, economic, and cultural problems. In addition, it encourages simplistic answers to complex questions and covers over the actual issues at stake when Christians seek to live their faith on this earth.

The argument supporting this contention will go back into history, for the way in which the paganization of Christianity in the churches came about can be appreciated best when viewed in an historical context. Then in part two I shall propose some possible means whereby historic Christian beliefs may be brought to bear upon the problems of a secularized (though not yet wholly secular) culture.

As I see it, some churches are presently wandering in the wilderness. Church leaders try to persuade their followers that the wilderness is their true home, the place where the real meaning of the gospel will appear for the first time. Church members know very well that something is amiss, but they are unwilling to question a leadership to which they have been accustomed to look for spiritual guidance. They are told how the old agenda for the church's mission was mistaken; it was narrow, otherworldly, and fundamentally unchristian; and now it has been brushed aside by the realities of the modern world. They sense, all the same, that the strange new agenda promises simply an endless journey towards an earthly utopia, a mirage receding constantly into the unimaginable future. They deserve something better. The prodigal churches have gone into a far country and there squandered their heritage. Having traveled so far from the Father's house they propose to go even farther, dragging along with them those in their care until the wilderness engulfs them all.

This is strong language and may seem exaggerated. It certainly requires some documentation. My next chapter considers the means by which the Christian gospel may be distinguished from other religious beliefs claiming to be Christian and applies this test to the strange new agenda.

2. Undeclared Myths and the Christian Myth

It was not any cleverly invented myths that we were repeating when we brought you the knowledge of the power and the coming of our Lord Jesus Christ. . . . As there were false prophets in the past history of our people, so you too will have your false teachers, who will insinuate their own disruptive views.

2 Peter 1:16, 2:1 JB

Everywhere the New Testament is blunt in its warnings to members of the church not to be diverted from the teachings they have received. Nothing is more important for believers than to understand "the salvation that we all share" and to confess "the faith which has been once and for all entrusted to the saints" (Jude 3 JB). False teachers are singled out for special condemnation.

The hymn "Tell me the old, old story / Of unseen things above," is hardly outstanding in literary merit, yet it explains adequately enough how people become Christians. They do so by hearing the Christian story. The story is "of unseen things above" because, though it largely speaks of persons and happenings on earth, its structure and meaning concern things that are not seen, namely, God's revelation of himself to Israel and his purpose in sending his Son to be Saviour and Judge of the world. The knowledge the story brings is revealed knowledge learned only through the mediation of the Holy Spirit who creates faith in the hearer. Such, at least, is the traditional Christian view based upon New Testament evidence.

In this view, false teachers are people who mislead the community of the faithful by retailing their own versions of the Christian story—cleverly invented myths. The use of the word myth (*mythos* in Greek) in this context points to the fact that though in the ancient world the word could mean simply story, it had long been used to refer to some legend or made-up tale. This usage was much the same as the common present-day usage. In ordinary speech, as we know, the word myth today means some belief or theory manifestly false. We speak of the myth of perpetual motion, or the myth of the master race. Just so, in the early church, the story derived from the Hebrew Scriptures and the apostolic preaching was clearly differentiated from the products of pagan imagination. The writers of the New Testament wished to make perfectly clear that the Christian story was based on actual events. It was not a tale spun out of somebody's head without any connection to historical facts.

Today, it is common enough to see the Christian story referred to as "the Christian myth." This usage began with nineteenth-century scholars in the field of comparative religion. These men regarded all religions to have originated in the pre-scientific imagination. Ignorant of natural laws and the nature of cause-and-effect in the world around them, primitive peoples made up stories involving supernatural beings, gods and demons (good and evil spirits), animal ancestors, and so on. Myths were the first efforts of the human race to acquire knowledge. They mixed observation and folk memories with pure imagination. They were essentially fabulous, although they often embodied in their fables some quite shrewd guesses concerning the nature of natural phenomena. And they explained the order of nature as they experienced it by telling stories supposed to have taken place in the remote past, in days when the gods mingled with men, begat children with women, and instructed tribes on how to acquire useful arts. In those days, it

11

was supposed, animals could talk, and fire, trees, and clouds were self-directing persons.

According to this reading of comparative religion, then, the Christian story was a myth like any other religious myth. It was a made-up tale belonging to the childhood of the race, one destined to be abandoned with the spread of knowledge grounded in scientific facts.

Nevertheless, religion still persists in our scientifically-conscious age. Today there is a return to the use of the word myth in the natural sense of story. It is becoming recognized that *all* beliefs rest upon stories taken to be true. Even beliefs derived from scientific facts belong in this category. The facts may be well-established. The constructions raised upon these facts, all the same, are products of the human imagination. No one can consider every available fact when building up a picture of reality. Theories that attempt to be all-embracing inevitably make their own selection of the facts, ignoring those thought to be irrelevant—which may actually be the most relevant of all! Beliefs are beliefs and cannot be made into anything else, however sophisticated or unsophisticated they may happen to be. They derive from stories we are told or tell ourselves, and unsophisticated stories may well be nearer the truth than sophisticated ones. But we have no means of telling objectively, since beliefs are necessarily subjectively received or adopted. On the other hand, beliefs are not wild guesses made on no evidence at all. Unless they are irrational or fanatical beliefs, they look at the world of experience and draw conclusions from it. The result is a believable myth.

Myth in this neutral sense is a useful word, provided it is clearly distinguished from the pejorative sense of myth as belief going contrary to the available evidence and therefore *un*believable. There is nothing intrinsically objectionable to Christian sensibilities in the phrase "the Christ myth," especially since the neutral sense is becoming much more frequently used. As always, meaning depends upon context, and the context can make plain that nothing derogatory is being implied when the Christian story is called a myth. There are times when it is extremely pertinent to speak about the Christian story without assuming it to be either true or false. In literary criticism, for example, critics will do so as a matter of course. Literature is the realm of stories, not of judgment about facts. Christians explaining the Christian faith *may* wish to do so. In addressing nonbelievers in this way, they are not ramming the truth of Christianity down unwilling throats. Instead they are saying, in effect, "Here is the Christian story. You do not have to believe it to understand it. It takes account of some factors in our existence not included in other beliefs about the nature and meaning of human life. Yet even Christians, who think it no fairy story but the plain truth revealed by God himself, do not imagine that it can be proven true. In the last resort, it has to be accepted by believing that God has given his revelation through Jesus Christ; or, as Christians say, it is to be received through faith."

I shall be using the phrase "the Christian myth" throughout his book for another reason. My purpose in writing is to explain how many kinds of teaching current among the churches in our day are not what they claim to be: the Christian gospel adapted to the needs of our generation. Rather, they are varieties of what the New Testament calls "another gospel," presented through "cleverly invented myths." Instead of arguing directly that these teachings are counterfeit versions of the historic gospel, I shall try to uncover the basic stories they tell about what it means to be human (as a popular expression has it). When this is done, then the great distance between these so-called contemporary Christian accounts of the faith and traditional Christianity stands out very plainly. By placing the Christian myth over against the new myths, they can be much more easily compared. For one thing, what the new myths imply but do not state in so many words is brought out into the open. For another thing, they can be seen to be not so very new after all, but largely variations upon nonchristian myths—some of them ancient.

When a particular set of beliefs is proposed for adoption, hardly ever (except perhaps in some books of philosophy or theology) is it admitted that a myth is involved. Thus it is important that any new agenda for the churches should be shown for what it is, namely, conclusions drawn from myth or story intended to explain the meaning of human life within the universe. The people anxious to update Christian faith usually talk as though they are proposing self-evident truths, truths which Christians not hopelessly bound to outmoded ways of thought must immediately adopt once they have been pointed out. They claim to be the champions of the genuine Christianity as opposed to what was called Christian but actually was the restricted outlook of former ages. So the myth underlying the thinking of these people remains undeclared—probably because they are wholly unconscious of its being there at all. Their conclusions are listed, while the reasons for these conclusions are not. The story line of a controlling myth has been suppressed.

Fortunately, even when a myth remains undeclared its outlines can usually be discerned. It can usually be pieced together by following the general exposition of the case being made to win the reader's assent, noting carefully the exact words being used and especially the metaphors. The exposition can then be cast in narrative form. For instance, the myth M. M. Thomas is using when he describes the mission of the Christian church must run something along these lines:

> After God had initiated the first stage(s) of his process of creation, man was endowed with spirituality. But this spiritual potential remained unrealized. Science and technology were rudimentary, poverty abounded, and submerged groups were denied participation in power structures. Then Jesus Christ came into the world. He helped to save the human spirituality by giving it a new orientation. But for two thousand years society advanced little towards becoming a fraternity of free and equal persons. Recently, however, a new stage of the creation process has begun. A new age is dawning. A revolutionary search for the just society is being carried out through movements of human liberation. The creativity recognized by Jesus Christ and present in him (and in other founders of world religions) is on the move. The church, which previously had only a preparatory mis-

sion, has now the chance to participate in the advance towards a society freed from oppression and underdevelopment.

This "new agenda" myth is necessarily of my own construction; yet I have tried not to distort Dr. Thomas's words unduly. Of course one would like to know better some details of his myth. What are his criteria for identifying the end of one stage in the creation process and the beginning of another? Did Jesus Christ reorient human spirituality solely by providing an example of loving service, or did he communicate his Spirit mystically to his followers? Did God merely set the creation process in motion and after that watch what humans would do with their spirituality, or was his indwelling Spirit ultimately the force urging the human race to its creative search? These unanswered questions, all the same, do not touch the core of the myth—its general drift is clear enough.

Obviously, this myth cannot be reconciled with the Christian myth. It is totally unlike the old, old story of Jesus and his love, which requires a framework of Creation, Fall, Redemption, and Last Judgment. Elsewhere, Dr. Thomas does speak of the Fall. But he identifies it with the selfish tendencies appearing at each stage of creation and assumes that human spirituality simply must face this as an obstacle to be overcome. Essentially, then, humanity is self-redeeming.

In the previous chapter I commented on the extreme abstractness of the new agenda and its remoteness from the actualities we experience. When put in the form of a myth, the agenda's unreality becomes even more evident. The name of Jesus Christ is the sole reference showing it to have anything to do with this earth. Otherwise, it might be science fiction describing some imaginary planet. The Apostles' Creed (which is not a telling of the Christian myth but a summary of highlights from it) finds it necessary to mention the Virgin Mary and Pontius Pilate. The old, old story cannot be told without including also Abraham, Moses, David, the prophets, John the Baptist, the apostles, and so on. Even supposing the Christian myth not to be true, it still is bound up with real people, real places, and real historical events. But the new agenda myth *looks* invented. Ignoring the complexities of actual human history, it tells an essentially *in*human (because impersonal) story of an abstract being called man today being spiritually oriented to search for a utopia. If this is the meaning and purpose of God's creation, it seems a somewhat futile story. Our planet seems to be going nowhere—for the word utopia, we may remember, means just that. True, Dr. Thomas does not use this particular word (though many sharing his outlook do). Yet his story ends as if he had done so—with a search which cannot possibly be guaranteed success. The sufferings of millions of the earth's inhabitants within previous societies are supposed to be justified simply because of what man today *hopes* to achieve. Meanwhile, anyone contemplating the present moment will see the poor and the oppressed in numbers never before equalled.

Undeclared myths stay undeclared because those who believe them prefer to use the language of other myths, silently changing the sense of the borrowed words to suit their own myths. Any such hidden myth, however, gives itself away all too readily. It declares itself by the presence of recurring words and phrases foreign to the language it has adopted. In the case of Dr. Thomas's new agenda myth, words belonging to the Christian myth—Creation, Fall, Sin, Salvation, and even God and Christ—appear changed in meaning either subtly or blatantly. Unalerted readers, seeing these Christian-sounding words, may well assume them to carry their familiar sense. One the other hand, when they see wording alien to the Christian myth—Human Liberation, Spiritual Creativity, Process—they are likely to experience at least a sense of unease. Expressions of this kind carry theological overtones; that is, they indicate some undeclared myth to which they properly belong.

These expressions or ideological terms are the gateways through which one can enter most easily the world of current myths disguised in the language of the Christian myth. I shall call them dogmas, because, like all ecclesiastical dogmas, they are particular articles of faith laid down for unquestioning acceptance by faithful believers. There are a multitude of nonchristian and secular dogmas around today, easily recognized since they are the current coin in the talk of progressive thinkers everywhere. We find them strewn around both in learned journals and in the mass media.

I shall now turn to look at some of these dogmas individually. My next chapter is devoted to the dogma of Inevitable Progress. This is a dogma so fundamental to devotees of the new agenda for the churches that they do not mention it, but simply assume its universal acceptance. Naming the dogma openly, moreover, would be to obviously "let the cat out of the bag." As an unexamined dogma it functions well. If once questioned, it might lead quickly to other dogmas dependent upon it to be challenged as well. The three chapters following the one on inevitable progress will consider four other popularly received dogmas: Man Today; Human Spirituality and Human Liberation (considered together); and Humanization. In the course of my survey of these five dogmas, the myths underlying them will emerge and declare themselves.

So far I have quoted only M. M. Thomas, taking his views as representative of a large number of proposals over the years for bringing the church into the modern age or bridging the gap between the church and the world. From now on, I shall be mentioning many names, present and past. My investigation requires some forays into history in order to understand better how the confusion among the churches concerning their mission and message has come about.

3. The Dogma of Inevitable Progress

Yet I doubt not thro' the ages one increasing purpose runs,
And the thoughts of men are widen'd with the process of the suns.

Alfred Lord Tennyson

Whether or not the thoughts of earth's inhabitants are widened as time rolls on, the focus of their thinking certainly alters. Today we may find it hard to believe that the word progress originally meant simply a journey. Since the one journey universally taken is the progress from the cradle to the grave, the thinking of our ancestors until at least the eighteenth century found its focus there. They did not expect the journey to alter significantly for future generations, as it had not for all the generations before them. The vital question was how to be equipped for proceeding on the journey. The age-old answer to the question had always been one word, wisdom.

For the Hebrews, everything in life revolved around obedience to the holy will of the living God. So wisdom began with the fear of the Lord (Ps. 111:10) and was found in the righteous life, a result of keeping his commandments. The Greek and Roman gods were amoral. Graeco-Roman society looked to philosophers and poets for guidance in living, much as our modern secular society looks to psychiatrists and the mass media. The early Christians inherited the Hebrew tradition of

18

wisdom, but this came through a Judaism partly influenced by Graeco-Roman culture. In the New Testament we can see the influence when the word virtue appears alongside the word righteousness and also in such passages as the one where St. James exhorts his fellow Christians like this: "Who is wise and understanding among you? By his good life let him show his works in the meekness of wisdom" (Jas. 3:13 RSV). Nevertheless, the New Testament always emphasizes strongly that the wisdom imparted by God is not of this world.

Central to New Testament teaching, however, is the declaration that in Jesus Christ a new revelation of God's purpose for human life has been given. By sending his Son into the world and raising him from the dead, God has shown that "in him lie hidden all God's treasures of wisdom and knowledge" (Col. 2:3 NEB). For believers in Christ's resurrection, the life lived in wisdom is no longer an end in itself but rather a preparation for life beyond the grave. The earthly progress has become an open-ended one leading to eternal life. Thus the preaching of the Christian myth transformed the ancient world, in which the fear of death was omnipresent. Instead of a shadowy half-existence in the underworld at best, individuals looked forward to being with the Lord. And as an end result of Christ's victory over death there was the expectation that creation itself would be "set free from its bondage to decay and obtain the glorious liberty of the children of God" (Rom. 8:21 RSV).

This picture of the human journey informed the imaginations of Christians down the centuries. When St. Thomas Aquinas, the most eminent among the philosopher-theologians of the medieval church in the West, spoke of the Christian being as a traveler *(viator)*, he was speaking of the progress towards heaven. There the blessed who on earth had walked by faith would see the triune God through the bestowal of the "beatific vision." And the best known exposition of the Protestant form of the Christian myth was itself a story about a traveler: John Bunyan's *The Pilgrim's Progress from This World to that which is to come* (1678). So long as the Christian picture of life was dominant, no one thought of progress as necessarily moving from the worse to the better or from the lower to the higher. In the eighteenth century William Hogarth issued a set of prints called "The Rake's Progress." The story told by Hogarth's drawings was of a life going downhill all the way.

Equally, the Christian hope for the restoration of a fallen creation to its original glory did not involve anything resembling progress in the modern sense. During the long centuries when the Western world was coming to birth, Christians universally believed that virtue had been declining since the time of the apostles and would continue to grow worse until the end times described in the book of Revelation. This conviction was based on the words of Jesus, "But when the son of Man comes, will he find any faith on earth?" (Lk. 18:8 JB). During the Renaissance, however, the cultured classes began to admire what human genius could achieve and questioned traditional pessimism over the future of humanity. The rapid rise of science and technology and increasing world trade in the seventeenth century increased the spirit of optimism immensely. With the eighteenth century came the first confident declaration of a new, wholly optimistic, vision of history.

Instead of being the record of a sinful race, doomed except for that portion of Adam's seed finding salvation in Jesus Christ, history was now defined as the story of an ascent. Humanity, slowly emerging out of the pit of ignorance, was rising to claim its birthright: the knowledge that brought power. The stages of the ascent were marked by successive historical eras leading up to the modern age, which has just begun.

Thinkers of the eighteenth century proudly announced that the new age was one liberating us from bondage to a past of superstition and misery. No longer was the virtuous life thought to be obedience to rules invented by the clergy, for now virtue would declare itself through the free use of reason. Throughout Europe it was proclaimed that the new age was one of "enlightenment"—*siècle des lumieres*—*Aufklärung*—*illuminismo*. As Immanuel Kant said in his essay *What Is Enlightenment?* (1784), the illumination of the human mind was an ongoing process, an emergence from the state of tutelage to full self-determination.

One aspect of the Enlightenment was pride in the new scientific knowledge. Alexander Pope, the poet who reflected so fully the contemporary outlook, wrote,

> Nature and nature's laws lay hid in night:
> God said, *Let Newton be!* and all was light.

Few thinkers of the period advocated atheism. Most took the path of Deism, adopting the belief that the Supreme Being governed the universe through the natural laws he had decreed and through the free agents he had created to be his delegates on earth. Science and reason together were thought to hold the key to the future, the one exploring the world around us and the other directing our actions. Human nature and its potential for good, therefore, concerned us most of all. In his "Essay on Man" Pope wrote,

> Know then thyself, presume not God to scan,
> The proper study of mankind is man.

Although Pope referred frequently in his poem to providence, following his advice meant ceasing to see one's existence on the context of an eternal destiny. The poem concentrated upon our obligation to live for the advance of the well-being of society and harmonious personal relationships.

Advocates of the Enlightenment invented some of the dogmas which today we accept and never question as true. The dogma of inevitable progress is chief among these. For the Enlightenment, knowledge was always increasing and so the future was bright. The enemies of change were the enemies of human good, for nothing held back universal improvement so much as holding to old ways and the beliefs of former, unenlightened ages. Set free the thirst for knowledge and trust human reason to regulate every sphere of individual and corporate life. Then the world *must* improve beyond all recognition. The dogma of inevitable progress, naturally enough,

21

rested upon a myth devoutly believed to be unquestionably true. This was the story of the human race finding its own way out of ignorance into knowledge.

In the eighteenth century, progress was believed to depend on ever-widening knowledge together with conduct regulated by *good sense*. Good sense was the yardstick by which all traditional institutions and beliefs were to be measured, in order that virtue might triumph in our behavior. This yardstick was applied, in particular, to the churches and their traditional beliefs.

Sometimes the verdict was wholly negative. Edward Gibbon's *Decline and Fall of the Roman Empire* (1788) drew a picture of an advanced culture destroyed by Christianity. Tolerance, urbanity, and good order (the virtues of Roman rule) proved no match for ignorance and blind fanaticism (the Christian mentality). Rome fell because it was weakened by the rise of Christianity. The result was the onset of the Dark Ages that for centuries stifled reason and perpetuated conditions of barbarism. For Gibbon, good sense could only declare that Christianity was the enemy of all that was most noble in the human spirit.

In this estimate many of Gibbon's contemporaries concurred. As Kant argued, hitherto Europe had been supine before the joint authorities of church and state. Now people were daring to think for themselves instead of being told what to believe. For many, Kant's views were amply confirmed by the French and American revolutions.

Nevertheless, Enlightenment thinkers recognized that religious beliefs had existed in all societies since recorded history began and possibly were as old as human consciousness. Some saw this as proof that religion belonged to the childhood of the race and would vanish as superstition gave way to scientific facts. But the majority saw it as indicating an essential human response to the mystery of existence. So, while eighteenth-century references to "our most holy Religion" were often ironic, they were not always so. There was widespread agreement with Gibbon over the sinister role played by the Christian churches in suppressing human freedoms ever since the Emperor Constantine had made Christianity a state religion. The usual accusation, however, was that the churches had perverted true Christianity, such as that in the Sermon on the Mount and the golden rule. The perversion had begun with the disciples of Jesus. Being men of their age, they had misunderstood their Master and tried to honor him in the only way they knew—by turning him into a god. In their primitive consciousness he was the loving Son who sacrificed himself to an angry Father and thus saved his followers from punishment in the afterlife. (St. Paul was usually considered the chief architect of this folly.) The Christian churches had then gone on to imprison the simple teachings of Jesus in a rigid structure of incomprehensible creeds and theologies.

In the name of *good sense,* then, enlightened opinion undertook to rescue the Christian religion by dividing Jesus from Christ, the teacher of timeless truths from the supernatural Saviour worshipped by adherents of a barbaric faith. In the next century, this separation was to be known as the need to choose between the options: the Jesus of history and the Christ of faith.

Jesus the teacher almost universally passed the test of good sense. He was a man ahead of his time. Had he not called himself the Light of the World (Jn. 8:12) and called on his disciples to be the same (Matt. 5:14)? Since education in the eighteenth century was based on the Greek and Roman classics, everyone was convinced of the need for cultivating virtue in order to achieve wisdom. So the teachings of Jesus were claimed to be in agreement with the findings of reason and to lead to true wisdom through the pursuit of virtuous living. Reduced to ethical conduct in conformity with the laws of the moral governor of the universe, Christianity was reinstated as an enlightened religion.

While the age of Enlightenment believed in progress in knowledge leading to the increase of virtue, it still took human nature to be a constant. Thus the superiority of the age to former ages did not mean that *nothing* could be learned from the past. True, the traditions of the past were mostly to be unlearned to clear the way for future emancipation of the human spirit. Nevertheless, Enlightenment thinkers continued to favor the notion that the best individuals of ancient times remained

23

unsurpassed in virtue, and so were models for the modern era: Socrates and Jesus, for instance. In politics as well, the statecraft of Greece and Rome deserved to be remembered, sometimes as a warning and often as an inspiration.

The age of Enlightenment wished to avoid anything that might be called mystical or metaphysical; "presume not God to scan" was a caution taken seriously. Consequently, it drew back from explicit theories about how God operated in relation to human reason. The age that followed felt no such inhibition. As the nineteenth century arrived, *good sense* began to seem shallow thinking. Eighteenth-century Deists too were criticized. With their absentee landlord God, Deists were seen as occupying a halfway house between old-fashioned supernaturalism and genuine atheism. Post-Enlightenment thinkers split into two parties, which may be called the materialists and the spiritualists. The materialists equated reality with facts proven scientifically, dismissing everything else as superstition. The spiritualists (not, of course, those people claiming to communicate with the spirits of the departed) held that reality was essentially spiritual and that the world explored by the sciences was no more than one aspect of the real world.

The latter party, made up largely of philosophers and theologians, was the one introducing the myth underlying most present-day reinterpretations of the Christian myth. I shall be detailing this myth and the dogmas it has spawned in my next three chapters. What is important to note here is simply that both parties accepted the dogma of inevitable progress—with a difference.

The materialists carried on the Enlightenment tradition of believing in progress as a visible fact. They pointed out that knowledge already had increased beyond all expectations. Progress was inevitable in the sense that, once human society had acquired a taste for knowledge, it would never be content to sink back into ignorance. Therefore, you can't stop progress. The spiritualists, on the other hand, claimed much more. For them (as I shall later show in some detail), spirit meant aspiration to the highest. Progress was inevitable because the human spirit could not deny its own nature. It was destined to soar endlessly upward, carrying with it the whole material universe.

The two post-Enlightenment parties, then, were polar opposites. The intellectual life of the nineteenth century was torn between them, with traditional Christians fighting on two fronts to defend their beliefs. Few people then were aware that one obscure intellectual, studying in the reading room of the British Museum in London, was working out a way to combine materialism and spiritualism. Karl Marx invented a myth which was to be the greatest challenge to the Christian myth since the rise of Islam.

Today we think of the Victorian era as a time of prosperous, complacent, moralistic, and unimaginative people with middle-class values and few, if any, doubts. Yet it was a time of turmoil, of actual and incipient revolutions, and of the erosion of traditional beliefs. Material progress was costly in human terms and left behind it a trail of troubled and anguished individuals.

In the eighteenth century people mostly either adopted enthusiastically the outlook of the Enlightenment or else they stayed content with traditional Christian beliefs. The Methodist Revival in England and the Great Awakening in America alike witnessed to the fact that, for large sections of the population, the Christian myth was still wholly satisfying. The nineteenth century saw a failure of nerve among the churches, in spite of their continued large following and the unprecedented expansion of their influence all over the world following the organization of foreign missions. For the churches, as for every other institution in the culture of the age, the mood was one of outward assurance and inward misgivings.

Alfred Lord Tennyson, Queen Victoria's beloved poet laureate, represented the cultural climate of his century much as Alexander Pope had done of his. The words quoted at the head of the present chapter show him supporting the dogma of inevitable progress. In the Christian myth, God's purposes are steadfast and unchanging; Jesus Christ is "the same yesterday and today and for ever" (Heb. 13:8 RSV). Yet here is Tennyson, a Christian at least in intent, speaking of an *increasing* purpose and widening minds. In the same poem ("Locksley Hall") he claims to have a vision of a coming earthly utopia. Yet doubt is omnipresent in his poetry, a black thread running through the golden tapestry. In melodious lines he voices the disharmony in the contemporary soul that wants both the fruits of ideas disturbing old certainties and these certainties preserved intact:

> Let knowledge grow from more to more,
> But more of reverence in us dwell,
> That mind and soul, according well,
> May make one music as before.

Tennyson's "as before" says it all. He asks for a progressive future in which everything stays as it was, only more so, a future where he can have his cake and eat it too.

Knowing that this is impossible, Tennyson tries to turn his doubts into a kind of meritorious religious affirmation, protesting,

> There lives more faith in honest doubt,
> Believe me, than in half the creeds.

This is a far cry from the days when Martin Luther, convinced that *his* doubts came straight from hell, threw his inkpot at the devil. Still, the presence of an intrusive "believe me" gives a clear signal to the reader that the poet does not actually believe what he is saying. So too, in connection with the declaration about an increasing purpose running through the ages, the overemphatic "yet I doubt not" suggests the opposite of a deep conviction.

Tennyson's poetry as a whole conjures up a picture of the poet pulling petals off a daisy and chanting, "I doubt, I doubt not, I doubt . . ." It is a picture of what the Victorian era has bequeathed to our age; a nostalgia for the days when the Christian myth gave meaning to the progress of our lives; and a bittersweet contemplation of our present situation. We realize that we have joined ourselves to science and technology and that divorce from that union is out of the question. For better or worse, we are yoked together and must continue our partnership wherever the progress may lead. Bunyan's pilgrim fled from the City of Destruction. We, less fortunate, seem condemned to wait and wonder whether the name of our civilization will turn out to be the same.

These considerations lead us back to the change in the word "progress." That words change their meanings, or go out of currency altogether to make room for freshly-minted words, is a fact of life. It is the condition for using language at all and a sign that our language is not dead. At the same time, noticing what old words go and what new words arrive is a good way of discovering what our culture believes worth talking about.

Something vital was lost when the word "progress" ceased to mean a journey and became instead the term used to describe development in society at large. What was lost in particular was concreteness. For progress in the modern sense is so abstract that it can mean anything or nothing. One person's progress can be another person's decline. Only the most crass evaluation of progress can be generally accepted as true in its own terms. We can grant, for example, that when a manufacturer of detergents brings out a new and improved product this is *real* progress (provided the advertisements can be believed).

The change in the meaning of progress was followed by the near loss of the words "wisdom," "righteousness," and "virtue." This is hardly accidental. The beliefs which these words communicated were made obsolete by belief in progressive advance through expanding knowledge and through the use of technology to make possible the good life. So today the remnants of words formerly considered to define that in which the good life consisted show merely contemporary disapproval of those values. The word righteousness survives almost solely in the epithet self-righteous and virtue in overly virtuous, or smugly virtuous. The word wise persists chiefly as a prudential term indicating knowledge of immediate cause-and-effect, as in, "Grandma, is it wise to wake the baby?"

The dogma of inevitable progress has been questioned

often enough in our century by people holding quite different sets of belief. If it still persists—and it persists prominently in particular among the leaders of some churches—this is because ditching the dogma would result in having to discard most of the other contemporary dogmas. For if we are not progressing towards an earthly utopia, where are we going? Once such a question is raised, an enormous gulf of doubt yawns at our feet. Perhaps, after all, we are not standing at a new stage in God's process of creation. Perhaps our progress is still stuck in the age-old journey from the cradle to the grave. Perhaps.

My next chapter seeks to inquire whether our present situation is genuinely unique. If it is, then we can still continue to believe that progress is inevitable because we are by nature progressive persons. If it is not, then we may have to start to recover some of the lost words which formerly guided our forebears in their progress through life.

4. "Man Today": The Dogma of the Contemporary Consciousness

The man of today . . . is not simply the man who happens to be a member of our generation but rather the man whose whole outlook is moulded by the present cultural situation and who, in turn determines, preserves, or transforms it. . . . This man is, even if he may be in actual count in the minority, the decisive spiritual type of our day. The tensions of his life represent a creative energy that is active in all spheres of life.

Paul Tillich

To be called a creative person is the highest compliment anyone today can receive. On every side we are urged to make all our activities *creative,* from marriage to microwave cooking. In the religious sphere the one thing needful is creative spirituality (or spiritual creativity). Among certain churches, such creativity is exhibited—so we are constantly told—when Christians try to bring about social change. Writing of his ideal Protestant Christian in 1951, Paul Tillich pictured him as "the man of today," the product of contemporary culture and active there, bursting with creative energy. Today, no doubt, Tillich's choice of an exclusively male model for the role might be thought sexist. His judgment concerning the qualities needed to be "the decisive spiritual type of our day" would still be approved.

Woman or man, such an individual has to have a genuinely contemporary consciousness and prove it by being always on the move.

In the ancient world, creative energy (as we call it) was regarded with mixed feelings. On the one hand, it was surely a divine gift and could accomplish great things. On the other hand, it was unruly, unpredictable, and potentially destructive unless directed wisely; and energy and wisdom seldom went together. The story of Samson among the Hebrews and of Achilles among the Greeks make this moral plain.

For both Hebrew and Greek, wisdom was the one gift without which every other gift miscarried. More than an individual gift, wisdom accumulated over the centuries resided in custom. Breaking with tradition was sometimes necessary, but always dangerous. Rather than being energetically on the move, then, staying with what was tried and tested was the wise course, unless there was every good reason for doing otherwise. "So then, brethren, stand firm and hold to the traditions which you were taught by us" (2 Thess. 2:15 RSV). The Christian gospel was founded on the traditions passed on by Christ's apostles and contained in the Scriptures.

Today, the idea of learning from tradition is foreign to us, for we are children of the Enlightenment. Yet it is certain that our whole culture would collapse tomorrow if we abandoned the traditions we have inherited from past generations and taken for granted. Family life, the institutions of law and government and education, science and literature, sports and recreations, public order and private civility, even the means of communicating with one another—all would go if traditions went. But we are conditioned to think tradition is stultifying. The daily increase in knowledge makes the ideas of yesterday obsolete. So we must break away from traditional ways of doing things. Be creative!

That the best of our creative acts may be foolish and misguided, if not dangerous, is not considered. The meekness of wisdom or humility hardly seems creatively energetic. Humility is another of those words almost extinct today.

Undoubtedly, there has been a notable retreat from the mood of the 1960s, when the young believed they had simply to tear down the old order to allow the age of unlimited freedom to arrive. Most of those who then demonstrated against the establishment have now joined it. The strong tide towards conservatism in politics continues to flow. Although tradition has not been reinstated by name, there is a renewed concern about preserving what has been inherited from the past.

Nevertheless, we continue to suffer from the disuse of words needed to express the values being reinstated. The present widespread anxiety over the environment ought to cause us to reflect upon our lack of humility before the intricate web of nature, remembering how confident we were only yesterday about our actions. Complaints concerning the growing indifference to the sanctity of life are fully justified. Yet what else could we expect? In our secularized society we say that everyone has a "right" to life. But we no longer speak about things being sanctified or holy. (Even among Christians, the word sanctification is hardly ever heard, except when the Bible is being read). Dismay over the patent failure of our schools to produce a minimum of literacy is a somewhat late-in-the-day reaction to a situation we ourselves have produced. For since knowledge became separated from wisdom and virtue, why should any child *want* to become an educated person? The sole incentive to gain knowledge is the prospect of an increased income or a position of power. The large numbers of those who have little hope of climbing to the top of the tree in industry, the professions, or politics naturally see education as a futile exercise. Education has lost its moral basis.

Having ceased to be the pursuit of virtue and the hope of achieving a measure of wisdom, the goal of life in contemporary culture has become the progressive satisfaction of our desires. The good life, if and when we reach it, will grant us what we feel we need, deserve, or have a right to. Thus we have not changed so greatly from the 1960s, when the slogan was, "do your own thing." This slogan remains largely the unspoken motive for living, whether contentedly within the establishment or rebelliously outside it. The unchecked growth of the drug culture shows the latter option to be increasingly attractive. The former option has created the class of persons currently called Yuppies, and it is seen in the political pressure exercised by special interest groups in order to obtain their human rights. The chief difference between our generation and that of the sixties is that the mob tactics of student revolt have given way to working within the system.

The reason why the body politic has not been torn apart by selfish interests, both individual and collective, is that most people today continue in traditional patterns of life: raising families; finding some degree of satisfaction in their daily work; relaxing with their friends; trying to act as responsible citizens by assisting in voluntary agencies, and perhaps also in local and national political life. If they belong to a religious tradition, they will say that their faith helps them in everything they do. Political engagement is not a top priority for the majority. Yet politics is important, because without it needed reforms in our collective existence would not come about. It is a part of all traditions to allow for reasonable change, without which society would stagnate. At the same time, all changes must be wisely chosen and implemented with care lest the attempt to drive out one devil admits seven others.

The errant churches, apparently blind to all these facts of everyday existence, are energetically getting rid of all their traditions. The cry has gone up that the man of today cannot believe in traditional Christianity with its outmoded dogmas. And so these churches have bowed down before the dogma of man today. That there is such a creature is a dogmatic pronouncement, for the sole evidence for it is that some people believe in it. How the belief in the abstract entity "man today" came about is an interesting story.

The Enlightenment saw the beginning of the idea that today was special. Advocates of enlightenment were certain that the latest generation was in an enviable position because it enjoyed all the benefits increasing knowledge had already brought. Some individuals in every generation would choose to remain ignorant and would fight against progress. But progressive thinking would prevail. Victory must lie with those trusting in the human capacity for self-determination. These people were the genuine representatives of today, while those trying to put the clock back represented a yesterday doomed to extinction.

It was left to post-Enlightenment thinkers to improve the notions of people with the mindset of today as contrasted with others wishing to call back yesterday. The thinkers I have called spiritualists deified the idea of the spirit of the age. They invented a myth explaining the growth of enlightenment from generation to generation by attributing the phenomenon to a universal consciousness present within humanity as a whole. This consciousness was always expanding. Tennyson lived at a time when the myth was widely accepted, and that is why he could speak of "an increasing purpose" running through the ages.

Individuals could be the bearers of the universal consciousness, but the consciousness itself was not their own consciousness—they could only manifest its presence. In any one generation, therefore, there were those who represented the universal consciousness most fully in its contemporary form. Through them "the decisive spiritual type of our day" (as Tillich terms it), revealed itself. The genuine man of today was not an individual existing alongside other individuals. He was merely the temporal and special locus of humanity in its latest manifestation.

A key figure in bringing the myth of man today into the Christian churches was Friedrich Schleiermacher, a professor of theology and pastor in Berlin. His book *The Christian Faith* (1821) was perhaps the single most influential work of theology produced in the nineteenth century. His earlier work *On Religion: Speeches to its Cultured Despisers* (1799) had profoundly impressed the young intellectuals of that time.

Schleiermacher rejected the outlook of the Enlightenment insofar as it had reduced religion to moral precepts. For him, the essence of religion was neither ethical teaching nor credal belief. It was rather our self-consciousness at its highest level. Religion awakened the human spirit to the possibility of taking divinity into itself, "just as did happen in Christ." Through religious experience self-consciousness became elevated into God-consciousness. While all religions led to a partial consciousness of our human dependence upon God, the Christian religion was religion in its fullness. It rested upon the complete God-consciousness possessed by Jesus Christ.

Religious experience came through *feeling*. In the eighteenth century, Jean Jacques Rousseau had declared our inner feelings to be infallible, explaining, "All that I feel to be right, is right; whatever I feel to be wrong, is wrong." Schleiermacher believed that feelings about right and wrong were to to be compared with feelings flowing directly from our consciousness of dependency upon the Universe-as-a-Whole or God. For he claimed that religious experience raised us up beyond ourselves as individuals to oneness with humanity, and so to the perfect union of humanity with divinity exhibited by Christ. Feeling was not simply trustworthy. It was the avenue leading from the finite world to the infinite.

In *On Religion,* Schleiermacher speaks about God as the Whole or the All or the Infinite; and he insists that every religious believer "must be conscious that his religion is only part of the whole." This suggests strongly that he is operating out of a myth other than the Christian myth. Indeed, in this work he lays out his own myth. He calls it "the Christian intuition," saying of it,

> It is just the intuition of the Universal resistance of finite things to the unity of the Whole, and of the way the Deity treats this resistance. Christianity sees how He reconciles the hostility to Himself, and sets bounds to the ever-increasing alienation by scattering points here and there over the whole that are at once finite and divine. . . . The Deity finds ever new devices. By his Power alone, ever more glorious revelations issue from the bosom of the old. He sets up ever more exalted mediators between Himself and men. In every later ambassador the Deity unites himself with humanity ever more closely, that men may learn to know the Eternal Being.

34

Certainly in the Christian myth sin is not the resistance of the finite to the infinite. That would make the created state sinful in itself. Sin is rather the claim of the finite to be infinite, if such abstract language is to be used at all. Similarly, where does the notion of a series of revelations of increasing value, and of "ever more exalted mediators," come from, if not from the dogma of inevitable progress? The New Testament witness is, "For there is only one God, and there is only one mediator between God and mankind, himself a man, Christ Jesus" (1 Tim. 2:5 JB).

Schleiermacher's myth tells the story of two worlds, the infinite and the finite. A channel of communication, religious experience, joins the lower world to the higher. The finite, by its very nature, seeks to block the channel. The infinite, however, contrives to keep it open and widen it. Resistance by the lower world to the power of the higher world is overcome by this power using as mediators those inhabitants of the lower world who at least somewhat successfully use the channel. Increasingly successful mediators guarantee that the inhabitants of the lower world will finally come to know that they belong essentially to the infinite and that their separate finite lives exist only for this knowledge.

In *The Christian Faith,* Schleiermacher sought to make the Christian myth fit into the framework of his own myth. This meant throwing out everything in the Christian myth that was historical (that is, events in the lower world) and all references to God having any direct dealings with our earth, except through human consciousness. God could not be called the Creator, for we know only of God being creatively active in our religious experience. The origins of finite existence are of no religious significance. The life, death, resurrection, and ascension of Jesus Christ are equally irrelevant to faith. Faith is the distinct impression we have of the man Jesus being also the Christ. The title "the Christ" simply designates this man as the one in whom God-consciousness was so complete that he represented humanity in its totality, and thus represents it eternally. Eternal life is not a gift; it is that which we always possess in virtue of our being at one and the same time finite and infinite.

Thus Schleiermacher separated *Jesus* from *the Christ,* faith from the reception of the Christian story, and God from the Father whose love for the world was shown in his sending his son to earth. The infinite, in fact, can love only the infinite. In *The Christian Faith* there is a section on "The Divine Love." Yet its conclusions can be summarized in this sentence from *On Religion* concerning the love of Christ, "Let us consider the living sympathy for the spiritual world that filled his soul, simply as we find it complete in him."

Having established the religious consciousness as the arbiter of all beliefs, Schleiermacher looked to the future and declared, "new ambassadors from God will be required" to awaken the spirit of Christianity "in a new and more beautiful form." No doubt, people who write a new agenda for the churches in our time believe that these ambassadors have arrived. The agenda is supposed to arise from the contemporary consciousness and to express the spiritual aspirations of man today.

After Schleiermacher there were other nineteenth-century thinkers who questioned his mystical approach to Christianity. (I shall be speaking about some of these in later chapters, since they have contributed to the current mix of teachings to be found among the churches). Few, though, departed from Schleiermacher's assumption that to be human was to be religious and that the issue was to find the kind of religion acceptable to man today.

The late-nineteenth and early-twentieth centuries saw a spate of books presenting versions of Christianity that claimed to be in line with modern thought, the modern mind, the spirit of the modern age, and the like. While often addressed nominally to "the cultured despisers of religion," they were intended at least as much to assure Christians that they too belong among the élite qualifying for the title of *the man of today*. During the fifties and sixties "contemporary man" was the favored phrase. Its nonsexist version, "the contemporary person," never became popular, although in the mid-sixties one essay at least (by Bishop Robinson) was entitled, "Can a Truly Contemporary Person not be an Atheist?" Perhaps the word "person" sounded not universal enough. A person has an individual soul, and what the Christ of man today saves is human spirituality.

Spirituality is the central concept of much of the thinking in the churches of our day, much as it was for Schleiermacher. He believed it essential to have the Christian story conform to contemporary ideas about consciousness gaining direct access to the spiritual world of the All or Eternal Being, even if it meant throwing out much of the story and reinterpreting the rest. That human spirituality and spiritual creativity are one and the same thing is a modern dogma. In the name of man today this dogma scorns the notion of learning from tradition or from anything not issuing from the contemporary consciousness. In my next chapter I turn to consider the dogma of human spirituality, together with the allied dogma that salvation through Christ must mean human liberation if it is to have any relevance for our generation. And I shall demonstrate that these two dogmas belong to a very ancient, though unacknowledged, tradition.

5. The Dogmas of Human Spirituality and Human Liberation: A New Gnosticism

What we have been considering is the second century of our era, and the reasons that led the Church of that day not to accept a new theology that professed to be in accordance with the spirit of that age. The Wise Man of old said there was a time for all things. That is true: the trouble is that people do not always have wisdom to know which in their time is the appropriate course.

F. C. Burkitt

One does not have to be a devotee of the dogma of the contemporary consciousness to wish to ask, "Is this the time to go back to the second century, when our concern is with the churches preparing to enter the twenty-first century?"

Well, perhaps it is exactly the right time. The New Testament shows us how the young churches of the first century were troubled by teachers who were substituting "cleverly invented myths" for the gospel taught by Christ's apostles. In the next century the trouble became acute. Many teachers called Gnostics or "knowers" were claiming to impart the knowledge leading to salvation *(gnosis)*, giving a true, contemporary interpretation of the way in which Jesus Christ had redeemed the world. After much conflict among the churches, church leaders known today as the Anti-Gnostic Fathers finally established a consensus that the teachings of the various schools of Gnosticism were incompatible with those handed down from the apostles. But for many years the issue hung in the balance. What made the Gnostics seem so admirable was that they presented their versions of Christianity in terms fitting the scientific outlook of the age. Their picture of how Christ became the world's redeemer agreed perfectly with the then up-to-date picture of the universe.

Many features of Gnosticism bear an uncanny resemblance to those of post-Enlightenment thinking in general, and to the themes I have been discussing in particular. The chief difference between second-century Gnostic dogmas and those current among us is that ancient Gnostics were not at all reticent in spelling out the myths underlying their dogmas—quite otherwise. Their beliefs were commonly presented in elaborate stories concerning the two worlds of the infinite and the finite, the spiritual and the material-historical.

Historically speaking, Gnosticism is a slippery phenomenon. The words at the head of this chapter are taken from F. C. Burkitt's *Church and Gnosis* (1932). Burkitt there claimed that Gnosticism began as a Christian movement, one wishing to express the faith of the church in language understandable to the cultured classes of the Roman Empire. During the half century and more since his book appeared, much more material has come to light, including important Gnostic texts. Yet the dispute about the movement continues, and especially about its origins. Christian or not, the movement had penetrated the Christian communities by the early years of the second century. Gnostic myths are very varied, but they have always had a similar view of salvation, even when they appear in later centuries. One variety of Gnostic myth is as follow:

The Cosmos has at its apex the Unknowable Supreme God of Light. The kingdom of Light was once invaded by a lesser deity, the God of Darkness. The Dark God captured sparks of light before he was driven back. He created the material universe to keep them in his power. For this reason, he is called the Demiurge or Workman.

The Dark God's creation was dual: Macrocosm and Microcosm. Each was constructed as a series of concentric spheres. The Microcosm's outermost envelope was the human body, enclosing the soul and—at the very core—a spark of captured light which was pure Spirit. The innermost sphere of the Macrocosm was the earth. Around it were transparent spheres containing planets and stars. So it is still, this creation familiar to us: each individual human being a microcosm structured like the Macrocosm, an evil creation.

In the fulness of time the Supreme God sent his Messenger or Son to the earth that he might rescue the imprisoned sparks of light. The Demiurge had stationed Lower Aeons (evil angels) at the boundaries of the spheres of the Macrocosm. When an individual spark was released by the death of its prison-body, the Aeons prevented its ascent to the Pleroma (divine fullness or Heavenly Society) whence it had been snatched. Similarly, they blocked any incursion from Above. But the Messenger tricked the Aeons, knowing their secret passwords, and appeared on earth. While there he remained free from the contamination of a body, though he seemed to have one. And he gave his *gnosis* to those who could receive it. Then he ascended, passing through the spheres, to take his place again with the Supreme God.

Since this visitation, the Messenger's gnosis remains available. It was passed on by a select group of his disciples on earth, who taught others of "the elect" to keep alive this teaching which was not for all ears. Today, all who awaken to self-consciousness of their essential nature as pure spirit are saved; and at death they also will rise through the spheres to the Pleroma. Yet, even now, they know salvation because they despise the prison-body and the Demiurge who made both Microcosm and Macrocosm and break all his tyrannical commandments. They also despise those earth-dwellers who have been born with no spirit at their core, though they pity their forlorn condition. But they seek to awaken "the elect" who are as yet unaware of the hidden spark within them. These sleepers must be awakened, or else the Demiurge will keep them as his willing slaves, afflicting them with all the torments he devised when he first designed this world as a place to keep Spirit from self-knowledge.

I have described this version of the gnostic myth at some length, introducing as many as possible of the themes found in different varieties of Gnostic teaching. For it seems to me that contemporary attempts to make Christianity acceptable to man today are understandable only when they are seen as a revival of ancient Gnosticism. For instance, M. M. Thomas's declaration that Christ is the Saviour of human spirituality makes no sense from the perspective of traditional Christian belief. Yet it makes perfectly good sense when it is read in terms of Gnostic belief.

Modern Gnosticism, of course, is not simply a republication of the old Gnostic myths, since it does not admit to having any myths at all. Instead, it claims to have discovered the real meaning of Christianity for our age. Nevertheless, this was precisely what the ancient Gnostics claimed to be doing when they told their myths! Modern Gnosticism has revived the themes found in second-century Gnosticism, but it has done so in the language used in our Western culture since the Enlightenment. In the ancient world, myth was recognized as a legitimate form in which to present philosophical truths of the highest order. Myth came down in the world after the Enlightenment, so naturally post-Enlightenment thinkers insisted that their teachings were no myths but fully compatible with the findings of modern science.

The best way to look at the whole issue is to begin by seeing where ancient Gnosticism diverged from the historic Christian tradition and why the church of the second century, in Burkitt's words, "did not accept a new theology that professed to be in accordance with the spirit of that age." What applied then may well apply today.

The Gnostic myth outlined above seems to agree in several important respects with the Christian myth, especially in regard to the descent and ascent of the Heavenly Messenger who was sent to bring salvation to human beings. But it disagrees even where it seems to agree. The crucial differences between the two lie in their understanding of the relationship between the earthly and the heavenly worlds. Three major points of differences stand out.

First, the Gnostic demiurge has the role played in the Christian myth by Satan. In Christian teaching the Creator is not Satan but the loving Father of the Redeemer of the world. At the same time, Satan appears in the New Testament as the one who tempted Jesus by offering him all the kingdoms of the world, and he is called the god or ruler of this world. Nevertheless, in the New Testament Satan's rule is that of a usurper. He is an intruder into God's good creation. The Anti-Gnostic Fathers fastened upon this point, insisting that the one Jesus called Father was the same God as Almighty Maker of heaven and earth revealed in the Hebrew Scriptures. They said he could fittingly be called the worker-God *(Theos demiourgos)*.

Second, in Gnosticism the human body is alien to spiritual reality. In Christian belief, God made the human creature a unity of body and spirit. In the New Testament the body is called a house or a tent because it is transient, but it is never a prison-house. Again, though it may seem that evil lies in the flesh and good is to be identified with spirit, the New Testament reference is always to the weakness of the flesh and not to any inherent evil in its composition. Jesus Christ came "in the flesh" (as the Gnostic Christ could not do without denying his heavenly nature). The resurrection of the body is a central feature of the apostolic teaching. True, the body will become a spiritual body in the afterlife, but this signifies a more perfect union of body and spirit than the earthly life knows. The risen Christ had flesh and bones and was no mere vision or spirit (Lk. 24:39).

Third, in the Christian myth eternal life is God's gift to his creatures. It does not reside in the essential being of humanity. The New Testament verse,

> "Awake, O sleeper, and arise from the dead,
> and Christ shall give you light" (Eph 5:14 RSV)

is probably a couple of lines from an early Christian hymn. Second-century Gnostics would have sung that hymn with gusto.

For them, it would have meant the spirit awakening to consciousness of its own nature, and of life in the body being spiritual death. For the Christian singer, on the other hand, the hymn would have meant Christ's dispelling the darkness of sin and his calling his disciples to the light of the gospel. In that light it could be seen that the finite and the infinite are not mutually exclusive, when God wills it otherwise. God has created finite being, but he has opened a way for his children to enjoy infinite bliss.

These three points of difference are to be found equally when we look at modern Gnostic teachings contrasted with traditional Christianity.

The dogma of human spirituality attributes all good in the world today to the creative activity of the human spirit. Yet modern Gnostics calling themselves Christians cannot speak explicitly of the God of the Hebrew Scriptures as the enemy of the God of Jesus Christ. Partly as a result of the work of the Anti-Gnostic Fathers, the Christian Bible contains the Hebrew Scriptures together with writings from the apostolic age; both collections being considered equally *Scripture*. Indeed, Schleiermacher said that the Old Testament should be an appendix to the New Testament instead of coming before it. He considered the religion of the Hebrew people to be a completely separate religion and its sacred books to be of interest solely because they were quoted by Jesus and the writers of the gospels and the epistles. Today, however, short of throwing out the Old Testament altogether, there is another course often followed in order to show disregard for the Creator. Christians with Gnostic leanings suggest that, until very recent times, the Creator did very little for humanity. Then he opened up a new stage in his process of creation, allowing humanity to start in earnest doing something significant to meet real human needs. This is M. M. Thomas's suggestion.

A somewhat similar course is to say that the Creator deliberately left his creation unfinished in order to leave room for human initiative. As William De Witt Hyde's well-known hymn puts it,

> Creation's Lord, we give thee thanks
> That this Thy world is incomplete;
> That battle calls our marshalled ranks;
> That work awaits our hands and feet.

Evidently the Lord was premature when on the seventh day he pronounced his whole work good and rested. Either he would not or he could not make it as good as it ought to be; so he left it to humanity to shout, "To battle! To work! Let's finish the job." The ancient Gnostics never tired of telling how stupid the demiurge was and how easily he could be tricked. Perhaps our latter-day Gnostics think that the best way to keep the demiurge quiet is to pay him compliments, thanking him for staying out of the arena in which humanity is perfectly competent to manage its own affairs.

The second point of Gnostic teaching, that life in the body is evil and a living death for the spirit, seemingly contradicts the whole modern Christian outlook. Is not the great complaint of traditionally-minded Christians just now that the Christianity of the churches has ceased being concerned with spiritual matters—the saving of souls and cultivating of individual faith— but has become preoccupied with people's bodies, their material needs, and with worldly issues in general?

Now, it is perfectly true that second-century Gnostics knew nothing of a progressivist view of the world. Like their Christian contemporaries, they had pessimistic expectations concerning the future of life on earth, and their hopes centered on gaining entry to a world beyond physical existence. Yet their contempt for life in the body was probably no greater than that found frequently today, in practice if not in theory.

The Christian tradition, holding that both our bodies and our souls are not our own but a gift from God, has never disregarded the body—though it places it far below the soul in value in God's eyes. The Christian life is lived out in the body, and the bodily needs of our neighbors can be ignored only at the risk of our own souls. What were called "corporal acts of mercy" in the medieval church were from the earliest days of the Christian church considered an essential part of the duty laid upon every believer, without exception. This duty extended from the nearest neighbor to the community in which one lived, so that concern for the righteousness of society as a whole could not become a neglected duty either. Nevertheless, knowing that the human world was a fallen world, Christians were well aware that fixing an ideal order for society in their minds and insisting that actual society lived up to such an ideal—*this* was no part of their Christian duty, but a failure to trust in the providential rule of the Creator and Redeemer. We were not called to play the part of God on behalf of our neighbor or of the generations coming after us.

What today is called "social salvation" is not simply helping actual people, here and now, to live lives of better quality and purpose and hopefulness. It means joining movements *promising* a more peaceful and prosperous life at some future date; or engaging in political action that brings advantage to one group of people at the expense or disadvantage of another group; or urging the adoption of some particular program for the sake of humanity—which is so abstract that it means nothing at all.

Part two of this book will be dealing at length with the subject of the Christian in society, so there is no need to expand on it at the present time. It is needful only to say here that the belief in the ability of human spirituality directed to changing the order of society is Gnostic in its contempt for the created order, including the human body. The present demand for the right to abort a human fetus regardless of the circumstances is an example of such contempt. The ancient Gnostics believed it a duty of the genuinely spiritual person never to bring another human body into the world. The reasons for choosing such a course have changed down the centuries, but the result is the same.

The third point of comparison between ancient and modern Gnosticism is the approach to eternal life. Gnostics saw escape from the prisonhouse of the body as liberation from the oppression of a tyrant demiurge. They would leave behind the limitations of finite existence and be raised to the pleroma or divine society of infinite freedom. The traditional Christian belief, on the other hand, was that perfect happiness and unbounded freedom would be found only with Christ in the world to come. Yet this did not mean exchanging limits for the limitless, the here-and-now for the All. In heaven, the triune God is still God and his children are still his children. God's will is always to be obeyed, even in eternity, yet now fully and without the pull of self-will to spoil the joy of obedience. This hope did not mean regarding the present world as a place of oppression. Nor did it mean abandoning earth to the rule of Satan. Yet Christians never have thought that the world could be turned into an earthly utopia or that even an approximation to any human ideal for society could ever be achieved. The limitations of earthly existence—even apart from the omnipresence of human sin—would prevent such a hope ever being fulfilled. What human betterment can be achieved will come about through people acting with as much wisdom as they possess and as much aspiration to righteousness as God may put in their hearts. Christian freedom is found in obedience to God's will. While we are on earth we have only an imperfect knowledge of all that God wills for us to do. But freedom in Christ means first and foremost the certainty of forgiveness when we choose wrongly and act unwisely. And we will continue to do both.

Liberation in the Christian sense is liberation from the power of sin—not from its effects. The modern idea that liberation means that people can and should demand to be set free at once from anything that they *feel* to be oppression is certainly more Gnostic than Christian. Even more clearly Gnostic is the belief that even though a particular group of people may not feel oppressed, if *we* think they are we must wake them up and convince them of the evil of their oppressed state. We are the knowers, and we are not going to let the demiurge get away with anything!

Later I shall be discussing the views of specific Christian liberationists. Here, merely liberation as a dogma is being considered. The idea of liberation, which embraces the idea of an earthly utopia, fits into the Gnostic vision of the world. Limitless freedom extended to every society and to every special interest group within society is the Gnostic pleroma brought down to earth. It is the finite raised to the infinite, sparks separated from the divine fire of the kingdom of light again reunited with their source.

Liberation looks like a secularized version of the Gnostic religion. Yet, in fact, it remains through-and-through religious—which is why it has been adopted so enthusiastically by many Christians today. Gnostics formerly pictured salvation in spatial terms: an ascent through the spheres to the pleroma. Now the picture has been altered to a journey through time: forward progress towards the earthly utopia. The faith of the Enlightenment in inevitable progress has been wedded to the spiritualists' faith in the human consciousness belonging to the whole, the unity that has overcome the resistance of the finite to the infinite.

Liberationism scorns the finite. This means that it scorns the earth and earthly existence. M. M. Thomas says that today's "creative search" is for a society that "eliminates poverty and oppression." Yet it is patent that an earthly society cannot legislate into existence an exact equality of wealth. If it does so theoretically, some will always find a way of beating the system, while others will suffer because of flaws in the system. If "the door of participation in power structures" is opened "to hitherto submerged groups," then the operation of these same power structures will inevitably submerge different groups and, very likely, in time the liberated groups will find themselves submerged again. By its very nature, power breeds inequalities and gravitates to the rule of the few over the many or to the dictatorship of a single individual.

Concluding that the second-century church acted wisely when it refused to accept a theology claiming to be the form of belief fitting the contemporary consciousness, F. C. Burkitt observed that people seldom have the wisdom to assess what is needed at a particular time. This lesson is written into history. Many individuals, hailed at first as liberators, have soon turned into tyrants. The orientation of the human spirituality to human liberation sounds impressive in the abstract. But when "brought down to earth," it means nothing more than an enthusiasm for programs that may do some good for a while (and even this is a large "perhaps"), but that soon may turn out to be disastrous. If by good chance they are relatively successful, they still will fall far short of expectations.

The lower aeons, the demiurge's evil angels, had the task of turning back spirits who tried to escape from the limits of prison earth. Today we are afraid of our own powers, powers that may destroy the earth either quickly or slowly. The limiting agent here is fear. As the fear of God is the beginning of wisdom, so our very human fears may teach us to *wish* to possess a little wisdom. It is hard for us, limited creatures as we are, to distinguish in any particular instance an unjust oppression from a justifiable restraint. Quite possibly, those whom we are ready to label oppressors standing in the path leading to liberation are not that at all. They well may be agents of the righteous God, stationed at strategic points to save us from ourselves. It takes wisdom to distinguish good angels from devils.

The dogmas of Inevitable Progress, Contemporary Consciousness, Human Spirituality, and Human Liberation are expressions of the belief that we human beings have no limits. These dogmas culminate in the all-inclusive Dogma of Humanization (variously referring to the humanization of the world, the humanization of society, the humanization of personal life, and so on). An examination of what this uncouth phrase is intended to mean will take us more fully into the *gnosticization* of Christianity.

6. The Dogma of Humanization

The hope which I seek is to be seen in "the sons of Abraham," who have executed an exodus from those religious and political estab-lishments which oppress the world today. . . . The front line of the exodus is not emigration, but liberation through the transforma-tion of the present. For in the present, where we always are, the powers of the past wrestle with the powers of the future, and fear and hope struggle for domination. By changing ourselves and the circumstances around us, by anticipating the future God, we emi-grate out of the past into the future.

Jürgen Moltmann

Through revolutionary change the *humanizing* of man and the *socializing* of humanity will be brought about, according to Jürgen Moltmann, a professor of theology at the University of Tübingen and the author of the influential book, *The Theology of Hope* (ET 1967). The words quoted above, explaining his per-sonal hope, illustrate his outlook. They illustrate also my con-tention that modern Gnostic myths differ from ancient ones in substance chiefly because they change the path to salvation from one ascending in space to one advancing through time. In each case, the purpose is to leave behind the here and now, the place where God has set us.

It is no part of Christian belief, of course, that God wants us to stay in the place where we were born. (Abraham is the classic instance of a reverse command.) No, the place of God's appointing is this earth, where we live in the concrete moments of the present as we make our progress until we die. But the old Gnostics thought their earthly existence to have been forced upon them by the Creator and his evil angels. The new Gnostics emigrate out of the past into a future that they, as individuals, will never see. Both sets of believers have been inspired by the same myth: a journey away from actualities in search of a realm of absolute perfection, one unlike anything we possibly can know on this earth.

The new Gnostics, when they claim to be Christian, have to find some means of avoiding the flat statement that the Creator is the evil demiurge. Jürgen Moltmann has found a device somewhat different from those I described in my previous chapter. He says God has not yet arrived but will finally make his appearance when his creatures have perfected this world. He is "the future God." In this way, Moltmann is able to absolve this God from all responsibility for the world as a realm filled with oppression and misery. Through his promises he is leading us from the miserable past to the glorious future. There is a problem here, though, as to how a being who "is not yet" could make any promises. Moltmann solves the problem by saying that it is God "in his eternal presence" who is still to come. In human history so far, God is both present and absent. His presence is to be found in humanity, insofar as humanity is *humanized,* that is, as it moves consciously towards the future. On this basis Moltmann can assert, "the story of God is the story of the history of man."

Schleiermacher said that the Infinite Being has scattered points over the earth that are at once finite and infinite. Similarly, Moltmann believes God is present in the realm of history (the finite) simply to the degree that humanization (consciousness of the infinite) is found. For Schleiermacher, the revelation of God's presence came in God-consciousness and was found in human religions, which contained ever more glorious manifestations of divinity. Moltmann changes the language from speaking of finite and infinite to one speaking of past and future. But since only some people in any era are humanized, Schleier-macher's image of the *scattered points* remains true for him also.

Ordinary mortals imagine human beings to be human beings. Why then it should be obligatory for them to be human-ized remains a mystery. It is because the process of humaniza-tion is a matter of *gnosis*—the Gnostic mystery or secret knowl-edge. Gnostics used to teach that not all human beings held within them the divine spark. Only the elect, the spiritual people *(pneumatikoi)* did so. Yet even these did not know of it until they were awakened to awareness that the earth was a prison and their present existence an exile. In exactly the same way, Moltmann teaches that becoming humanized is an awak-ening to the truth that the present (where we all live) is not our home, but that we are people in search of the human future which is the future of God. The basic Gnostic myth remains un-changed. Merely the imagery used in the telling of the story has been updated to make it acceptable to man today.

Thus the old Gnostics said that human existence lay under the oppression of the demiurge. Spirit-people showed their lib-eration from this oppression by ignoring the commandments of the tyrant Creator. The new Gnostics say that humanized people "execute an exodus" from oppressive establishments. (For the old Gnostics, too, the institutions of church and state were the manifestations of the demiurge's rule over the world). The old Gnostics saw this earth as the fortress of the demiurge and the lower aeons, their last stronghold in the eternal battle between the forces of light and darkness. The new Gnostics see the present as the place where the powers of the past wrestle with the powers of the future. Christians, Moltmann asserts, have no lasting city here on earth, "but their hope is not directed towards another better land—rather toward another new fu-ture for all countries. Therefore they do not emigrate from one land to another throughout the expanses of the earth, but throughout the vast eras of history."

Now the cat *is* out of the bag! For Christians, like other people, are limited to their earthly progress—though they hope for eternal life in the world to come after death. That is why they confess that "here we have no lasting city, but we seek the city that is to come" (Heb. 13:14 RSV). And they very definitely have their hope directed towards another better land, "a better country, that is, a heavenly one" (Heb. 11:16). Because they live on God's earth, all they *see* of history is a small section of the era in which they live. They learn from others about the past. The future is in God's hands and entirely unknown to them. When Moltmann speaks of Christians emigrating out of the past into the future, then, he speaks spiritually and describes not an earthly journey but a Gnostic one.

For the old Gnostics, the human spirit journeyed through the spheres to the pleroma. For the new Gnostics, the journey is throughout the vast eras of history to the future God and his eternal presence. Apart from dogmatic belief, there is no evidence at all for the reality of either of these journeys.

There is no evidence, either, for the reality of heaven as stated in the Christian myth. But Christian belief does not write off the present. Gnostics, new or old, believe salvation to be escape from the present with its sufferings and oppressions. Christians believe it to be living in the present assured that Christ has triumphed over sin and death. "Behold, now is the acceptable time; behold, now is the day of salvation" (2 Cor. 6:2, RSV). The hope of "a better country" may be a powerful incentive to seek salvation, but not more than a subsidiary motive for embracing it. The gospel promise of eternal life is the promise of life in communion with the eternal God both on earth and in heaven. Gnostic salvation, on the other hand, is tied to the promise of complete liberation from the bondage of this earth as we know it. That is why Moltmann, in his *Theology of Hope*, wishes to substitute hope for faith. The one thing needful in Gnosticism is the *gnosis* permitting emigration from the present; in Christianity it is the faith enabling believers to pray, "Thy will be done on earth as it is in heaven." The difference is the difference between getting what we want and asking what our Creator wills for us.

Christians regard the earth reverently. Although spoiled by sin, it is still God's good creation. Thus they also value the past highly, believing that in human history God has revealed his will for us who live upon the earth. Jesus Christ lived upon the earth, and Christians look back in history saying, "*There* and *then* salvation was brought to us." The old Gnostics identified their deity by calling him the alien God—the one alien to everything belonging to this earth. The new Gnostics call upon the future God, one revealing himself unambiguously only when the earth we know has run its course and is no more.

Moltmann is probably the most widely influential theologian since Tillich. Karl E. Braaten, who records his indebtedness to both thinkers, follows Moltmann's general perspective when he writes that the coming theology "will not go from above to below, but from the future to the present, for the sake of mediating the new into history, and creating a new tomorrow through revolutionary transformation of the world." In Braaten's words there is evidence again of the Gnostic revulsion from the thought that there is anything *above* us to which we owe allegiance or anything in the past which might teach us wisdom in coping with the present. The Gnostic watchword is "down with limits and down with continuity." Braaten even rejects the view that Christians should participate in politics. In his view, politics is suspect because it is too much bound up with continuity. It is not revolutionary enough.

Schleiermacher said that he hated religion being understood historically (e.g., when Christianity was called the offspring of Judaism). For him, Christianity and Judaism were eternally distinct types of religion flowing from different types of God-consciousness. So too, he saw no significance in the earthly life of Jesus. As a pioneer teacher of the new Gnosticism, he was still groping for the right language in which to express his doctrines. He still spoke in terms of the opposition between the finite and the infinite, which was more appropriate to the old Gnostic myth of the journey to the pleroma by way of the spheres. He thought of history in the eighteenth-century manner: a record of persons, places, and events—all finite. The thinker who was to forge the key terms for the new Gnosticism was his contemporary, a professor of philosophy in Berlin when he himself was there as professor theology. Georg Wilhelm

Friedrich Hegel taught the nineteenth century to bow down before history as the sole and sufficient revelation of God and his activities. In so doing, he laid down the groundwork for the dogma of humanization in our century.

Hegel's universal history or world history claimed to have grasped the real meaning of history in its totality, presenting final truth about the universe in an all-embracing speculative system. Thus Hegel was the first of the nineteenth-century spiritualists (as I have called them). Spirit was the source and the goal of all things. At first Absolute Spirit stood alone. Through its inner dialectic it developed matter, its opposite, out of itself. The result was the beginning of what we call history. A dualism of matter and spirit was illogical—contrary to the essence of Spirit—so matter and spirit found union in humanity. Spirit (God) thus became self-conscious in the human spirit.

Hegel was the theoretician of the new Gnosticism, as Schleiermacher was the religious guide. For instance, while Schleiermacher saw no evidence in religious consciousness for belief in the Christian trinity, Hegel taught that his threefold dialectic gave an infallible philosophical basis for this doctrine. During the later years of the nineteenth century Hegelian thinking influenced the English-speaking churches greatly, yet almost always through individual intellectuals. Schleiermacher's influence was both earlier and more pervasive. (Because the two thinkers disliked each other, they never got together to issue a common program for Christianity). Around the time of World War I, Hegel dropped out of popularity with both philosophers and theologians, returning to favor in the 1960s. At that time "radical Christianity" was the phrase used by Christians who believed themselves to be truly contemporary persons, and to appeal to Hegel's writings looked daringly innovative. Moltmann's *Theology of Hope* contains more references to Hegel than to any other thinker.

Nevertheless, Hegelianism never dropped out of sight altogether. At the turn of this century the most hotly debated question was "the Jesus of history or the Christ of faith?" Christian thinkers who followed either Schleiermacher or

Hegel insisted upon the Christ of faith. For Schleiermacher had taught that Jesus was really irrelevant to the Christian religion, since Christ or divine-humanity was what Christian God-consciousness affirmed. And in Hegel's system, Christ was the material universe itself awakening to self-consciousness through union with spirit. The Jesus-of-history school, on the other hand, carried on the Enlightenment tradition of Jesus as an individual man, the greatest teacher in history. This school had by far the greater popularity in the churches, since its understanding of Christianity was not of *doctrine* but of practical living, the Christian journey being one of walking in the footsteps of the Jesus who taught us to love and serve humanity.

In the early twentieth century, when Hegel's universal history was beginning to seem old-fashioned, a covert Hegelianism spread in the form of Process Philosophy. Process thinkers—those believing God's creation to be an evolutionary process—were considered to have brought together the Jesus of History and the Christ of Faith by showing Jesus' teachings to be an important step forward in the evolution of the religious consciousness. Alfred North Whitehead became a much talked-about name among the Christian intellectuals of the twenties. Whitehead said in his *Religion in the Making* (1927) that the Judaic concept of God was that of an Eastern tyrant, while Christ (his preferred term) showed that God worked through *persuasion,* drawing humanity after him to new, creative adventures in world-making. Whitehead's Gnostic myth declared itself at the end of his book, when he wrote:

> The universe shows us two aspects: on one side it is physically wasting, on the other side it is spiritually ascending.
>
> It is thus passing with a slowness, inconceivable in our measures of time, to new creative conditions, amid which the physical world, as we at present know it, will be represented by a ripple barely to be distinguished from non-entity.

The old Gnostics believed that we had to rise beyond the spheres around the earth to free ourselves from the curse of matter. Whitehead assures us that we have only to wait for world history to run its course and the curse will fade away.

Process thinkers brought into circulation the word "creative" to refer both to conditions within the process of creation and to human activities furthering the advance of the process. They also invented the word "humanization." Here the leading figure was Teilhard de Chardin.

Teilhard, the Jesuit paleontologist, was exactly twenty years younger than Whitehead. Because of the ecclesiastical ban on the publication of his writings, however, his name was virtually unknown as a process thinker until the first enthusiasm for the movement had subsided. When his books began to come out in the early sixties, they sparked a new interest in the movement by Christians, and also renewed Christian interpretations of Whitehead. For Teilhard, ours is a universe of evolving spirit, for "a universe whose primal stuff is matter is irremediably fixed and sterile." The universe, in fact, is *fundamentally and primarily* living, and its complete history is ultimately nothing but an immense psychic exercise; the slow but progressive attaining of a diffused consciousness." In Gnostic fashion, Teilhard defines progress as an "escape" from material existence; and, like Whitehead, he calls it a slow escape. However, since the time of Christ's appearance in the universe, all things are progressing towards *hominization* and *unanimisation* (Teilhard's own terms).

Process thinkers have a fondness for inventing new words (Whitehead invented a dozen or more), but Teilhard scattered new words on almost every page and had an equal fondness for italics. Calling the universe "a machine for progress," he saw Christ as the center of the evolutionary process, between the Alpha of its beginning and the Omega point of its ending:

> To be the alpha and omega, Christ must, without losing his precise humanity, become co-extensive with the physical expanse of time and space. In order to reign on earth, He must "super-animate" the world. In Him henceforth, by the whole logic of Christianity, personality expands (or rather centers itself) till it becomes universal. Is this not exactly the God we are waiting for?

The culmination of the process of super-animation is to arrive at "'a cosmic point Omega' of total synthesis."

Post-Hegelian philosophers were accustomed to describe Hegel's three-partite dialectic as one of thesis, antithesis, and synthesis. So we can see how Hegelian Teilhard's outlook is even though he may have little acquaintance with Hegel's writings. The word "humanization" has existed before, but there can be little doubt that, in Teilhard's latinized form of *hominization,* avant-garde Christians of the sixties found exactly what they needed: the concept of humanization. Those already turning back to Hegel would rejoice when Teilhard spoke about the evolving universe having "by its very structure" to "emerge into the absolute," through the agency of "mankind as a whole, collective humanity." Because we were entering "an entirely new phase of the race," Christ ought to be "*reborn* . . . in a way adapted to our present needs." The universe had gone through the stages of unconsciousness, consciousness, and self-consciousness. It was now poised to enter "the vast realm of the Ultra-Human." Christ as collective humanity would shortly achieve the perfect unification of the earth called *unanimisation.*

Unanimisation, said Teilhard, would be inspired by a vision of "some sort of transhumanity at the ultimate heart of things." Thus the old Gnostic myth lives on. The human spirit, awakened to *gnosis,* knows itself to be destined to final union with the pleroma. Process thinking in all its forms carries within itself an intimation of the self-salvation to be realized in humanization, since divinity is no more than humanity raised to its complete perfection beyond the divisions of space and time. John B. Cobb, Jr., who calls himself a Whiteheadian, writes that he finds the various types of liberation theologies incompletely developed, "but I can hardly doubt that it is in these forms that theology today has authenticity and vitality. We cannot move towards global salvation without hopeful images of the future, and no image is hopeful which does not picture all groups as able to shape their own destinies." Evidently,

Cobb sees no conflict at all between the idea of salvation and the idea of shaping collective destinies.

In the Christian myth, the son of the almighty Father came not to humanize the world but to save it by rescuing its inhabitants from the power of sin. In my next chapter I investigate what has happened to the traditional teaching about sin when it is transposed to fit into the framework of Gnostic myths of self-salvation; why, in its new setting, sin is judged unimportant; and what is thought to take the place of sin as the chief impediment to salvation through humanization.

7. From Sin to Creative Unhappiness

I danced on a Friday when the sun turned black—
It's hard to dance with the devil on your back.

Sydney Carter

The Cross still stands. . . . But this on one condition and one only:
that it expand itself to the dimension of a new age, and cease to
present itself to us as primarily (or even exclusively) the sign of
victory over sin—and so finally attain its fullness, which is to be-
come the dynamic and complete symbol of a universe in a state of
personalizing evolution.

Pierre Teilhard de Chardin

Whenever the Christian myth is told, sin is spoken of. For the story of our salvation through the cross of Jesus Christ is a story about God's grace and human sin. "And you shall call his name Jesus, for he will save his people from their sins" (Matt. 1:21 RSV).

Yet today in certain churches, sin is either played down or else left out of consideration altogether. The new liturgies adopted by the denominations illustrate the trend to eliminate references to sin from public confession and to substitute instead simply the admission that God's people have not always lived up to the best that was in them. Theologians too identify sin with the failure to be truly human and therefore with not having been sufficiently active in promoting social change.

The wish to take sin out of the Christian myth is not recent. It has a long history. And it is no mere indifference to whether sins are committed or not—the idea that sin is not particularly important. It is a definite hostility to sin as a concept. In this chapter I shall trace some of the patterns of thought resulting in an intensified hostility over the years to having sin remain a part of Christian faith. This will take us back to the eighteenth century.

John Wesley told the Christian myth by preaching what he called "the grand scriptural doctrines" in a culture welcoming the myths of the Enlightenment. No academic theologian, he wrote nevertheless a full-length theological work entitled *The Doctrine of Original Sin, according to Scripture, Reason, and Experience: in Reply to Dr. Taylor* (1756). Taylor, a Doctor of Divinity at Oxford University, had written a book on Original Sin in which he took the position becoming popular at that time. The human race, he argued, was not so much guilty because of some sin committed by its first parents but rather was imperfect. From the first, the deity had no wish to sit in judgment on his children but, rather, to guide them in the path of virtue. Wesley instead wrote his reply to "provide some antidote against that deadly poison, which has been diffusing itself for several years through our nation, our Church, and even our Universities." He noted that Dr. Taylor's "smooth, decent writings" were the productions of one

> who does not *oppose* (far be it from him!) but only *explain* the Scripture, who does not raise any difficulties or objections against the Christian revelation, but only *removes* those with which it had been unhappily encumbered for so many centuries!

Wesley was quick to recognize the pattern of thought adopted by the "friends of religion" in the age of Enlightenment. This pattern was to continue—at least in its smoothness, decency, and ostensible respect towards Scripture—up to the present. Dr. Taylor's belief that a loving God could not possibly be also a God of judgment is one with which we are perfectly familiar in our age. But more radical patterns of hostility towards the concept of sin were to follow. Dr. Taylor's transformation of sin into imperfectly developed virtue simply followed from his having accepted the dogma of inevitable progress. Had he known Alfred North Whitehead would write *Religion in the Making* a couple of centuries later, he might have called his book *Virtue in the Making*.

The Post-Enlightenment age followed, and Schleiermacher identified sin with the resistance of finite beings to the unity of the whole. What we call sin was not of direct concern to God, because it was simply some blockage on *our* side in the channel of communication linking earth to the realm of the Infinite or All. Imperfect God-consciousness made problems for us. Yet it was a transient phenomenon, destined to be overcome by the arrival of ever more glorious revelations of divinity, as more exalted mediators appeared with their religious teachings. With Schleiermacher sin had become relatively unimportant. But it was Hegel who made the whole concept of sin seem irrelevant.

Being a philosopher, Hegel was not interested in sin, only evil. The supreme reality being spirit, there could be no real evil in the universe. (Here he and Schleiermacher were at one.) Yet, in the second phase of the dialectical process, spirit and matter became estranged. At the point where matter first became self-conscious in humanity, what we call evil entered in the shape of the unhappy consciousness. Though unpleasant for us, the unhappy consciousness was the driving force behind all consciously-directed or willed progress. It generated the energy needed to push world history onward until a complete synthesis of spirit and matter could be achieved. Then all vestiges of estrangement or alienation would vanish.

Hegel's view of evil as both necessary and wholesome was carried on in the spiritualist schools of the later nineteenth and early twentieth centuries. It also came into Marxism. Karl Marx had taken over Hegel's dialectic but had "turned it right-side up" by substituting the material world process for Hegel's evolution of absolute Spirit into self-conscious spirit. For Marx, the class struggle was the embodiment of the unhappy consciousness. The coming of worldwide socialism would mean what Teilhard has called unanimisation. The goal believed by Teilhard to be progressive humanization culminating in union with the cosmic Christ was for Marx one to be reached finally with the arrival of the classless society and the withering away of the state.

Nineteenth-century theologians saw Hegel as an ally because he supported the idea of a universe ruled by spirit over against the skeptical tendencies of the Enlightenment tradition, which by their time had largely passed from Deism into atheism and materialism. By the end of the century the issue most widely debated in the churches was this: the Jesus of history or the Christ of faith. Supporters of the Christ of faith included both traditional Christians and those who believed Hegel to have provided the definitive form for Christianity to take in the modern world. Supporters of the Jesus of history were followers of the most influential theologian since Schleiermacher, Albrecht Ritschl. In the nineteenth century, Germany was the center of all progressive philosophical and theological thought.

Ritschl was in many respects the heir of the eighteenth-century Enlightenment, carrying on both the belief that religion was essentially moral teaching and the conviction that scientific enquiry must supplant traditional ideas based on superstition or mere speculation. But he was a theist, not a Deist; and he developed the eighteenth-century theistic view of God as a God of love. Viewing the Bible historically, he saw Jesus as a man in line with the Hebrew prophets. In the eighteenth century, virtue was thought to lead to *social virtue*. For Ritschl, Jesus saw his vocation as preaching the kingdom of God, or "the organization of humanity through action inspired by love," and so the mission of the church was to follow its founder. *The Christian Doctrine of Justification and Reconciliation* (1870), Ritschl's most important book, explained that Jesus had removed wrong ideas about God. Understanding that human wrongdoing came through ignorance, God had no anger against sin but forgave sinners freely.

The death of Jesus upon the cross redeemed us because it was a fitting end to a life spent in selfless dedication to the kingdom. Sin was self-seeking, and this could be removed by loving. The doctrine that Jesus himself was wholly sinless could not be proved, yet it was a helpful belief if it led us to see that Jesus was to be valued as the perfect revelation of the Father.

Because Ritschl's teachings seemed (and were meant to be) wholly practical, they spread widely among the churches. Until the 1950s, when people spoke of liberal Christianity they were referring to the legacy of Ritschl. Some liberals told the Christian story in fairly traditional terms. Yet nearly all of them held to three explicit dogmas: that the fall of Adam and Eve was a "fall up" into adult responsibility; that Christianity was the religion *of* Jesus (his faith in his heavenly Father) and not a religion *about* Jesus (as a heavenly being); and that the teachings of the Bible were acceptable only when they lived up to what *we* believed to be the moral standards of Jesus himself.

Ritschlian theology inspired the Social Gospel movement, with its program of reform through participating in democratic political institutions. Especially in the years immediately following World War I, many of the clergy left their pulpits to enter political life—in order to "advance the kingdom."

For liberal Christians, then, sin was once again real. But it was wholly manifested in actual moral evils, especially in social and political structures causing human misery. Liberal Christians did not curse the demiurge, because they thought creation could be redeemed through moral effort. I have already quoted from William De Witt Hyde's hymn "Creation's Lord." Hyde was an American professor of ethics of the social gospel period, and his hymn anticipates the Theology of Hope in its vision of the future. Still, it is actually a Theology of Will, for Hyde ends his hymn thus:

> What though the Kingdom long delay,
> And still with haughty foes must cope?
> It gives us that with which to pray,
> A field for toil and faith and hope.

> Since what we choose is what we are,
> And what we love we yet shall be,
> The goal may ever shine afar,—
> The will to win it makes us free.

In the period of widely diffused Ritschlianism social action was the program, but individual will was the spur to advance the kingdom. And Hyde's hymn illustrates this well. The enemies of progress too might be seen in corporate organizations or political regimes. Yet behind these there were always human faces. The "haughty foes" were people rather than powers.

It took a change of perspective upon the created world— and a new approach to sin and evil—to bring in the theologies of hope and of liberation which have dominated the thinking of the churches in recent years. Only the new approach is not new at all. It is simply a return to Hegelian thinking, largely influenced by its Marxist offshoot. In other words, it is a return to Gnostic myths.

Gnostic belief was wholly deterministic. It was purely a matter of destiny whether or not one was born with the divine spark within and when would come the awakening needed to be ready to take the journey back to the kingdom of light. No divine spark, of course, *could* ever be lost eternally since by its nature it was eternal. Modern Gnostics agree with their ancient counterparts. Schleiermacher pointed out the futility of petitionary prayer. The All could not be changed in the minutest respect by anything finite. For Hegel the only will was the world will. He used to laugh at who imagined world history could be deflected from its path by so-called "individual choice." Marx taught that freedom is the recognition of necessity. Religion reduced to ethics, on the other hand, has to believe in the freedom of the will. Ritschl looked back to Kant for his understanding of individual responsibility in the service of the kingdom. For Kant had taught that the undoubted fact that we are morally conscious beings proved the existence of freedom, God, and immortality.

If the social gospel, then, reduced the traditional Christian view of sin to wrong choices made through ignorance, the theologies of world evolution, hope, liberation, and politics rule out any concept of sin from the start. This does not mean, of course, that the exponents of such theologies have ceased to speak about these things all the time and with great passion. But sin in the sense of disobedience to the will of God is something impossible for them even to consider.

The impossibility of the Christian view of sin is perhaps best explained by looking at one of the foundation myths of the modern age, *Faust,* the epic drama by Wolfgang von Goethe. One of the literary landmarks of European culture, this work also openly challenges the traditional Christian perspective on human existence. Its influence has persisted to the present day to a greater extent than is commonly recognized.

Goethe's *Faust* was more than sixty years in the writing (1772-1831). It is founded on the old folk tale of an aging scholar who sells his soul to the devil in exchange for youth, love, and power. In *The Tragical History of Doctor Faustus* (1588), Christopher Marlowe had taken the German story and made it illustrate Christian belief in salvation through the cross of Christ. Though considered in his day a heretic, Marlowe used his play to portray most powerfully the consequences of a willful rejection of Christian obedience. Goethe's poetic drama, on the other hand, celebrated the self-confidence of a man possessing the cosmic secret that salvation came solely from consciousness of the eternal within himself.

Faust begins with a prologue in heaven, where God allows Mephistopheles to tempt Faust to fall away from righteousness—an obvious and intended parallel to the opening of the Book of Job. Faust does not sell his soul to the tempter. Instead, he makes a wager with him. He will live his life without once wishing a single moment of it to endure forever. Only once, as it turns out, does this nearly happen. Faust has built an ideal community upon a swamp he has drained. He pauses to think about the human happiness he has created. Then Mephistopheles thinks he has won the wager. Yet, in fact, Faust has not rested from well-doing; he has merely imagined himself participating eternally in the stream of humanity forever actively moving forward to new heights of achievement. So Faust is taken up into heaven, a paradise of perpetual creativity. Mephistopheles is seen as stupid in agreeing to the wager in the first place.

Gnostic themes abound in Goethe's work. Early in the drama, Faust explains that two souls lie within his breast: a higher soul seeking eternal activity; a lower soul seeking rest and ease. The higher soul is the exact equivalent of Gnostic *spirit,* yearning for the highest heaven of light. The lower soul is the Gnostic soul (psyche), satisfied with life in the prison house of the demiurge's providing. Then the swamp which Faust drains is earthly creation. A swamp was a common Gnostic image for this world, because a swamp pulls us *down* into it. Mephistopheles tempts Faust with every variety of pleasure, all in vain. Any Gnostic aware of possessing spirit does not accept the flattering and deceitful gifts of the demiurge. During the course of the drama, Faust's experiences lead him into fornication and manslaughter and results in the woman he loves being executed for killing their child. A pure Gnostic knows that the values of this world and its oppressive laws do not apply to him, so long as he loves with a spiritual love. Finally, it is when he is old and blind that Faust does his best work. A Gnostic draws upon himself the special enmity of the demiurge and his co-horts, and by enduring this with indifference he grows the stronger in spirit.

Yet to the old Gnostic themes Goethe adds some of his own. Again, early in the drama Faust is seen reading the prologue to John's Gospel. He is dissatisfied with the rendering of the Greek word *logos* as "the Word." Inspired from within, he cries triumphantly, "In the beginning was the Deed." Later, by building his humanized city upon the swamp, he puts his discovery into action. The old Gnostics had taught that the possession of *gnosis* could save them from being drawn down into the swamp and that it would raise them to life in the pleroma. Faust, too, is finally raised above, but not before he has made the earthly swamp into an earthly utopia.

The deed, the embodiment of the world will, is what the new Gnostics added to the old Gnostic myths. The creative energy of the human spirit, now so widely accepted as the one thing needful for man today, is indeed closely linked to the old Gnostic image of the spark from the eternal fire shedding the eternal light. Fire is the recurring emblem of energy for the human imagination—and has been so ever since people worshipped the sun as the greatest of the natural powers. Confidence in the potency of the spark-bearers is the contribution of new Gnosticism to the world of today. The new Gnostics not only defy the demiurge before they escape from him, but they also make use of his territory for the purpose of humanization. To second-century Gnostic Christians it had seemed sufficiently daring of the Christ to have descended into the enemy's heartland (the nation worshipping the creator) and there to have spread the knowledge of salvation. They had not counted on the inevitable increase of human creative energy that would make the deed creatively productive even upon the earthly marsh.

William Blake, the English poet, raged against the moral *good sense* of the century into which he was born. Without ever having read a line of Hegel, he invented a version of Hegel's dialectic. In "The Marriage of Heaven and Hell" he says, "Without contraries is no progression . . . Good is the passive that obeys Reason. Evil is the active springing from Energy." Evil or energy provides the new Gnostic's way to heaven on the hell of this earth. Thus, for example, Moltmann gives no explanation of why, in the present, the powers of the past and the future wrestle (see p. 49). Yet it can only be because the past is energy spent and the future is energy as yet untapped. In the same way he speaks of fear and hope striving for domination. Fear is that which would prevent the deed from becoming effective, while hope is the awareness of the destiny decreeing that the deed *cannot* fail.

Blake's poem, usually called "Jerusalem," was adopted a long time ago by the British Trade Union movement as a kind of secular creed. Gathered in Trafalgar Square in London, the crowd of workers sings,

> I will not cease from Mental Fight
> Nor shall my sword sleep in my hand,
> Till we have built Jerusalem
> In England's green and pleasant Land.

Presumably, no one ever stops to ask, "Why *mental* fight?" or notices the *arrows of desire* in the previous verse, together with burning gold sword and chariot of fire. Yet Blake's invocation to creative energy to end the present alienation of the human self from the eternal spiritual society or human totality is the meaning of the poem. In like fashion, Christian congregations join heartily in singing Sydney Carter's "Lord of the Dance." (The old Shaker tune provided for it is joyful, as Parry's tune for "Jerusalem" is stirring.) The verses seem to be telling the story of the birth, life, resurrection, and ascension of Jesus Christ. Yet they make much more sense when read as the work of creative energy making every finite moment in human existence dance to the tune of the infinite harmony which is so lacking on this earth.

In the lines quoted at the head of the present chapter, Carter's energetic Christ on Good Friday is still able (though with difficulty) to maintain the rhythm of his own dance: "For I am the dance / And the dance goes on." The alienation of the individual conscious-self from the spiritual whole creates an unhappy consciousness. Yet this alienation is still the only way in which spirit can reach total self-consciousness. There being no progression with without contraries, the human spirit must learn to bear the dead weight of material existence and still move forward with creative self-abandonment in order to be born anew to possess itself fully. Faust must never rest for a single moment. It is dangerous even to pause for an instant to contemplate the bliss of being fully conscious of one's union with the All once humanization has been perfected. In the present, where we all live, suprahuman and subhuman forces wage their war. But our present lot is always to endure the unhappy consciousness, so that our painful self-division may generate the energy for the next creative advance.

So, in the Gnostic myths, old or new, evil is part of the process of self-creation. Even the demiurge is a tool in the hand of the supreme God, since without his tormenting oppression the sleeping spirit might never awake to consciousness of being earth's prisoner. In the Christian myth, the cross of Christ is the place where human sin stands openly and is judged by a righteous God. And, on the cross Christ bears the guilt of our sins and we are pardoned. But also, in the light of the cross sin is seen to be the one evil which can never be good.

In the liberal view, sin is only our mistaken good intentions. So Jesus, by suffering to the death, gives us an example of how to live better, living for others rather than for our private happiness. In the Gnostic view, a literal cross has no place. The ancient Gnostics knew that Christ, never having taken on an actual body, could not have died. But they used the cross as an emblem of division, marking the material realm from the spiritual one. After all, this is where Christ stood when he appeared on this earth. It is fascinating to see that Teilhard de Chardin used precisely the same image when, objecting to the cross being seen as a sign of victory over sin, he wrote, "It [the cross] marks and must continue more than ever to mark the division between what rises and what falls back." The one difference between the old and the new use of the word cross as a boundary or dividing mark is that the new speaks in terms of progress and regression instead of in terms of spirit and matter. In the end, of course, there is *no* difference, for Teilhard believes, "All that exists is matter becoming spirit." It need not be any cause for surprise, either, that Teilhard sees no evil in pain unless we feel diminished by it—that is, lose our creative energy. Unhappiness is the spur driving us on to creativity.

Although with the growth first of liberal Christianity and then of new Gnostic myths sin has almost vanished from the vocabulary of the Christian churches, denouncing evil has not. This is the subject which I shall consider in my next chapter.

8. A Strange Commandment: "Denounce Your Enemies!"

"God, I thank thee that I am not like other men, extortioners, unjust, adulterers, or even like this tax collector."

Luke 18:11 RSV

Think of people oppressing others by denying their humanity; of life lived only in terms of appetites; of all that defiles human dignity and single-minded love. Lump it all together and call it sin. What else might we include?

from a Bible Study in a study booklet
Jesus Christ Frees and Unites issued by the
World Council of Churches, 1975.

Christians who have long ceased to think of sin as anything except an old-fashioned way of talking about sex outside marriage are somewhat embarrassed when they have to say what sin means to them. Because the word is so omnipresent in the Bible, it sometimes happens that they are forced to give their own views about why there is any point in continuing to use it today. On such occasions the best they can do is to identify the kinds of behavior they disapprove of and say that these might be classed as being sinful. Yet the notion of there being such a thing as *sin* distinct from *sins* eludes them. Talking of sin in the singular can only be a figure of speech referring to behavior that is blame-worthy because it is either foolish, or selfish, or anti-social, or all of these. And it is not a very helpful way of speaking, even then.

In the Bible many behavioral acts are called sins. Yet they are all variations upon one central act: defiance of the holy God. Sin means departing from God's revelation that we were created to love our Creator and honor his commandments. Whatever our *sins* may be, their common root is our failure to fear God and walk in the paths of his righteousness. The Bible invites us to turn from our sins and live. This invitation is for us first to admit that we are ruled by sin and then to accept the freedom of the people of God. Acceptance of the message of freedom *from* sin, nevertheless, is conditional upon repentance *for* past sins. God forgives us freely, but not after the manner of some popular books on psychology, saying "I'm O.K., you're O.K." So, after Jesus had commissioned the twelve, he sent them to preach the gospel. "So they went out and preached that men should repent" (Mk. 6:12 RSV).

As a gnosticized thinking has spread among certain churches, Christians have absorbed—most often uncon-sciously—the belief that there is no sin in our world. There is pain and unhappiness, and often individuals are to blame for in-creasing these evils. Yet, even more often no one human being is really to blame. Rather the social and economic systems we live in (together with the impersonal structures they require in order to function) are responsible. So, a common argument runs, sup-posing we stretch a point and agree to using the outmoded word "sin" to characterize human selfishness, ill-will, and careless-ness—that covers only a small part of the evil rampant in our world. We have to turn to the realms of economics and politics to find solutions for the major sins afflicting us. It is social sin and not individual sin that ought to concern us most today.

This argument contains a lot of muddled thinking—so much, indeed that I shall examine it a piece at a time.

First, let us agree that the contemporary world is looking for how to root out or lessen current evils, and that it finds talk about sin unhelpful. The reason for not calling in the word "sin" when discussing any evil is a sound one, and Christians ought to agree with it. The reason is because every evil causing pain, unhappiness, and even death is two-sided. On the one hand, all these evils are things we consider *bad* and want to get rid of. On the other hand, evils are *good* in that they keep us busy and well-occupied in trying to get rid of them. They are a kind of list of "things to be done" we draw up for ourselves. We make such lists every day at home: "Mend the dripping faucet; find out why the new T.V. set has not been delivered; remember the 2:00 p.m. dental appointment." We would rather not have to do any of these things, but we are the happier once they have been done. What applies in small affairs applies in great ones also. Pollution of the atmosphere, world hunger, or military coups in Latin America cause great anguish and fear, and demand action on the part of people of good will everywhere. Yet, these "haughty foes" also reveal "a field for toil and faith and hope." Today some Christians are told when they go to church that the true worship of God is service given to the world. They must engage in social and political action to bring about a just society; they must work to remove inequalities; and they must see that human rights everywhere are respected. For this activity is what loving your neighbor as yourself means in the contemporary era.

Certainly, Christians ought not to sit with folded hands and say that all these worldly problems are not their concern. Equally, they should not forget the nature of all evils under the sun. However urgently they call us to right palpable wrong, they are relative evils. While we are trying to right one wrong, we are leaving other evils to multiply—which may be much greater evils. Our efforts to do good may be disastrous, just as our domestic efforts to repair the dripping faucet may end in flooding the basement and having to call in the plumber.

The almost universally accepted term "social salvation," then, is a misnomer. The best anyone can attempt in connection with current evils is some social engineering. Christians can do more than that. From the perspective of nonchristians, the fact is irrelevant that their motive for trying to help is obedience to Jesus' command to love their neighbor. That motive is personal. What matters is whether they are of any help or not. Even if they are successful beyond their wildest dreams, some time in the future people will be saying, "We know those people back there thought they were making things better. Now *we* have to clean up the mess they left. Their so-called reforms may have seemed like progress in their day. But look at the evils they brought about which need never have been allowed to happen."

Social salvation is a possible combination of words only when what is relative (as all social, economic, political, and cultural conditions are) is turned into an absolute. And that is what the new Gnostics do. In part two of this book I shall be dealing with the Christian tradition and the answers this tradition provides for the questions concerning the Christian within society. At the moment my argument concentrates upon the consequences of accepting the view that today Christians should be busy dealing with social sins. My conclusion is that the secular world is perfectly correct in not wishing to hear the word "sin" brought into any discussion about social evils. Christians ought to demand that it never should be allowed there.

A second point is that Christians never should have allowed the word "sin" to have become so blurred that it became confused with the presence of evils in the world. The advocates of the social gospel are here very much to blame. By identifying God's kingdom with society organized through love, they brought in the wholly unbiblical notion of building the kingdom. The Christian who prays "Thy kingdom come, thy will be done on earth" should never add "through our efforts." In the Bible the kingdom is always God's gift and its coming hidden in his secret counsel. Social gospel teaching pointed to the social concerns of the Hebrew prophets and to Jesus as sharing their concerns. Yet it would be hard to imagine Amos or Isaiah standing for public office as so many social gospellers did, and voting with the National Reform Party of Israel or Judah. The prophets called for righteousness in the divided kingdoms, and they denounced kings, priests, and wealthy citizens for their disobedience to God's commands to act justly and mercifully towards the poor. They did not try to alter the social and political structures of their day, any more than Jesus did in his day.

Christians since the sixties, however, have heard less about the liberal ideals of the social gospel than about the absolutist ideologies of the Hegelian tradition, including its Marxist offshoot. Liberation theologies belong wholly to the latter tradition. This trend has greatly increased the danger—always present in any theory of social salvation—of identifying the Christian gospel with one brand of political thinking to the exclusion of all the rest.

When Christians look upon a particular set of social evils as being *the* evils to be removed at all costs, then other Christians failing to agree with them are likely to be called unchristian. Some of God's commands pertain strictly to our individual relationship with him, while others involve our dealings with our neighbors. The Great Commandment, as it is called, states this truth succinctly: we are to love God *and* neighbor. It is unfortunate (to say the least) then, when no clear distinction is made between sinning against neighbor-love and tolerating some social institutions or political systems in spite of the fact that they contain manifest evils. What is involved here is wisdom. Among relative choices to be made by mortals, the question to be asked always is, "At this time and in this place, which one of two courses is the wiser to take?" The wiser will inevitably be the more loving. In political life, the situation is no different from that in private life where (let us say) parents are told by a doctor that a dangerous operation may save their child's life. Decisions are hard, and to leave the decision for another to make sometimes may also be wise rather than cowardly. For one Christian to tell another that he or she is not a Christian and is lacking in love because of differences over social salvation is itself a wholly unchristian act. And it does not matter whether the differences are over specific political programs or over the decision by one of them not to engage directly in politics.

This brings me to my third point, which is the one I wish to develop in the present chapter.

From a secularist viewpoint, the word sin is an anomaly in

today's world. Christians may accept the fact with patience, though not with any kind of mental ease. But when Christians begin to use the word in such a manner that it is evident they themselves do not know what it means, then the situation has become intolerable.

The extract from a World Council of Churches booklet at the head of the chapter illustrates how bad the situation has become. The statement I have quoted puts in simple terms a viewpoint to be found often (expressed in tortuous language) in academic theological books as well as in pamphlets and magazines distributed by denominational headquarters. I have paired it with the words of the Pharisee in the parable of Jesus, because the similarity between the two is startling. In the booklet we are urged to *think of people* doing all kinds of obviously sinful things because they are things which we ourselves disapprove of. The only real difference between us and the man in the parable is that we do not happen to have a handy tax collector standing beside us at whom we can point an accusing finger. We at least think of ourselves as those who wish to uphold human dignity and practice single-minded love.

Even the classes of persons singled out for contempt in the two passages are fairly similar. The Pharisee's list is extortioners, the unjust, and adulterers. The modern list is oppressors, the unspiritual, and defilers. The old phrase for adultery was "defiling the marriage bed." But today adultery is hardly considered worthy of being called a social sin, while offending against human dignity is a sin almost deserving the penalty of stoning.

It is instructive to see how closely, too, the modern list of things that people should not sin against corresponds to the qualities Goethe bestowed on his Faust. Lump all the episodes of *Faust* together and call its hero sinless! He is the exemplar of single-minded love, a man wholly dedicated to making the future of humanity free from oppression, and fully human. He is all these things because his higher soul would not allow him to live his life in terms of appetites.

Instructive also, in another connection, is how Mephistopheles in *Faust* has a bearing upon the nature of evil, now so

75

frequently called *sin* by Gnostic Christians. No devil to be feared, he announces his function in the drama by saying, "I am the spirit that always denies." In other words he plays the same role in relation to Faust as the antithesis in Hegel's dialectic plays to the thesis. He brings Faust to full self-awareness by bringing him into situations that test his endurance and the steadfastness of his hope. Without the unhappy consciousness his tempter brings to Faust, the latter would not have been raised finally to the heaven of unending energy.

Now, it is "the spirit that always denies" that makes the Christian liberationist, for example, so happy in unhappiness. Without the spur of believing in the misery of those languishng under oppression, no champion of liberation theology would join movements or publish this type of belief as the final truth of the Christian gospel revealed to the contemporary consciousness. It matters not at all whether the examples of oppression chosen to show the need for liberation theology are situations where the oppression is actual and appalling or where there is virtually no real oppression at all. The strength of the belief does not depend upon facts of history but upon internal conviction, based on feeling. Yet, without any presence of the denying spirit—some consciousness of oppression being out there in the world—liberation theology would have died soon after its birth in the brain of the first theologian to identify political liberation with the Christian faith.

The liberationist also needs the denying spirit embodied in individuals or groups, for there can be no just war without an unjust enemy to be attacked. The old Gnostics believed that here on earth they took part in the eternal warfare between light and darkness on two fronts. First, there was the assault of the demiurge and his angels; and then there was, besides this frontal assault, the attack from the rear by human agents of the demiurge. Similarly, modern Gnostics see their battle as involving cosmic powers—past and future, fear and hope, reaction and progress—and human enemies under the domination of the *status quo* or spirit of the past. Attacking the human enemies is a religious duty. Their utter sinfulness has to be exposed.

The liberationist theologian Paulo Freire has laid down

three main conditions for entering the Christian life. He calls them annunciation, denunciation, and conscientization. The first is receiving the gospel of liberation and its hope of a humanized future. The second is identifying establishments standing in the way of the arrival of the future. The third is the individual Christian's resolve to remove from himself or herself all vestiges of the "oppressive consciousness." Freire's three conditions correspond to the traditional Christian terms: receiving faith, confessing one's sins, and receiving sanctifying grace. The liberationist version of Christianity no longer believes that God in Christ creates repentance in the Christian so that faith in the redemption achieved by the cross of Christ is accepted and the path to sanctification opened. Instead, we do it all. *We* accept the new gospel. *We* confess other people's sins. *We* work upon our own consciousness to make ourselves sinless.

It is a frightening prospect for the future when denouncing one's enemies becomes an essential part of being called a Christian. For in effect the liberationist Christian has claimed to be able to represent, here and now, the Christ of the last judgment. This Christian is empowered to say, "Depart from me, you cursed, into the eternal fire prepared for the devil and his angels" (Matt. 25:41 RSV). Anyone who has failed to "execute an exodus" out of those oppressive establishments named and denounced by this Christian is automatically among the damned.

Readiness to categorically denounce others hardly comes under the heading of "speaking the truth in love" (Eph. 4:15 RSV). According to another liberationist theologian, Gustav Gutiérrez, the gospel message is about "the continuous creation, never ending, of a new way to be a man, *a permanent cultural revolution*" (his italics). So perhaps denunciation is a way of showing love for the revolution if not for one's neighbor. A famous play of our century, Jean-Paul Sartre's *No Exit*, contains the line, "Hell is other people." For the new Gnostics hell is all the people who do not agree with them. Thus the only way in which a gnosticized Christian can visualize the meaning of sin is to keep all such wicked people in mind and say, "Look there—*that* is sin. I thank God that I am not like them."

9. The Triumph of Abstract Thinking

What liberates is the knowledge of who we were, what we became; where we were, whereinto we have been thrown; whereto we speed, wherefrom we are redeemed; what birth is, and what rebirth.

"The Valentinian Formula," quoted by
Clement of Alexandria (c. 150–c.225)

Jesus appeared among the Jews. He appeared possessed of a new spirit entirely his own. . . . Had the spark of life lain dormant in the Jews, he would only have needed a breath to kindle it into flame and burn up all their petty titles and claims . . . but though the Jews did want something different from what they had had hitherto, they were too self-satisfied in the pride of their servitude to find what they sought in what Jesus offered.

G. W. F. Hegel

Hegel had started out as a theological student. The quotation given above is from a monograph (unpublished in his lifetime) entitled *The Spirit of Christianity and Its Fate*. Written before he had invented his philosophy of absolute spirit developing through world history, this early work shows Hegel believing that religion holds the key to unlock the mystery of life. In these years he defined religion as "the self-elevation of man from finite to infinite life." *The Spirit of Christianity* seems especially old-Gnostic, because in it Hegel contrasts the spirit brought by Jesus with the Jewish belief in God as sovereign Lord. Jesus, says Hegel, knew that the spiritual consciousness dwells in God and finally returns to the Godhead. Thus Gnostic imagery abounds in the monograph as it describes the life of Jesus in terms of a Gnostic journey. In the few lines I have quoted can be seen the *spark* of the divine fire; Jesus *appearing* rather than existing; and the *servitude* of worshipping a God above.

For Hegel, the fate of Christianity was to founder on worshipping the individual man Jesus rather than the spiritual reality which Jesus found within himself and sought to teach others to know. The whole Gnostic tradition, from the earliest days to the present, *hates* anything having to do with the concrete events of history—just as Schleiermacher said. In other words, it hates this earth. Only abstract ideas—and especially the idea of the Whole or the All—delight it, for what is farthest away from our day-to-day existence *must* be true. Jonathan Swift, the great eighteenth-century satirist, believed the reverse. He wrote,

> I have ever hated all nations, professions and communities, and all my love is towards individuals. . . . But principally I hate and detest that animal called man; although I heartily love John, Peter, Thomas, and so forth.

Swift was a Dean in the Church of England. He also was a sincere Christian in an age growing increasingly skeptical. Perhaps he never spoke so well in defense of his faith as here.

The Christian and the Gnostic myths are alike in having to be received in faith, for neither can be established through tangible evidence. They are unlike in that Gnosticism is a faith invented by human thought. On that ground, Gnostics have claimed to reveal the highest, the secret wisdom of the unknown God. Only a knowledge coming into this miserable planet where all is oppression and pain could speak of ultimate reality. Such knowledge must have come from the realm of light where the unknown God dwells, shining in the human spirit which itself is a stranger here, having come from above.

Valentinus of Alexandria (d. 160) was a second-century

Gnostic who seems to have begun his career as an orthodox Christian. The Church Father Clement of Alexandria, who was once his pupil, has recorded the formula (or short creed) which Valentinus composed after he became a teacher of his own brand of Gnosticism. The formula traces the Gnostic journey by which the soul, originally from above, is forced against its nature to endure earthly existence until the time that it receives *gnosis* and can be reborn and return to its original home. The image of the soul being thrown forcibly to earth, incidentally, has been revived in our own day by the German philosopher Martin Heidegger. "Thrownness" was the term Heidegger used to describe what he called our being-in-the-world.

What is most interesting today about the Valentinian formula is its declaration that salvation means liberation—an unlimited liberation, because, of course, anything belonging to the Above or the All can have no limits. It is this abstract, absolute quality of the concept of liberation that causes so much mischief when liberation is identified with the modern Christian version of freedom in Christ. For although the Christian myth begins above, with the almighty Lord, it descends at once to earth. The supreme God is not an unknown God, for he creates our universe and enters into relationship with it. He reveals himself to individuals, to Abraham, Isaac, Jacob, and Moses. He speaks through the prophets and at last through his Son, sent to earth to save his people. And he continues to guide the church of Jesus Christ by his Holy Spirit.

No one hearing the Christian myth can overlook the obvious fact that many of the themes it contains look very much indeed like themes found in Gnostic myths. The theme of the heavenly messenger descending to this world and ascending again is the most central of these themes. But other themes, such as the struggle between light and darkness, or reference to the god of this world, point the same way. It would be extremely surprising if large similarities did not exist. Even if Gnosticism is a much older form of belief than Christianity, it was certainly very prevalent in Christian communities very early in the second century. The example of Valentinus shows that some Gnostics were previously well-regarded Christians. Many words and ways of describing the world found in both Gnostic teaching and the New Testament, besides, were common in the Graeco-Roman culture and had no special tie to any religious belief. They were used in astronomy and philosophy and in the ordinary speech of the time. Then, the fact that some beliefs found in Gnosticism are mentioned in the New Testament is not complete proof that they were peculiar to Gnosticism. For instance, in the New Testament 1 John attacks an apparently current denial that Jesus had a body, insisting that Christians confess that Christ has *come in the flesh* (1 Jn. 4:1-4). This may simply reflect the low regard in which the body was generally held in Greek thought, indicating that some cultured converts had brought their ways of thinking with them. On the other hand, Gnostic teachers may have been already active in the church. We simply do not know, one way or the other.

Some scholars have argued that St. Paul and St. John *were* Gnostics, or at least near to the Gnostic ways of thought. Yet this is hardly a plausible conclusion. The use of certain words found widely in many Gnostic systems as technical terms proves nothing. St. Paul used the word conscience, which was a word invented by the Stoics. The fact that St. Paul found it a convenient word to use does not make him a Stoic. The crux of the matter does not lie in whether certain words or phrases occur in the New Testament. It lies in how they are used. In every case we find that the New Testament use is to assert God's close relationship with the earth and earthly existence, while the Gnostic use is to insist on no connection between the finite and the infinite.

A clear example is the antithesis between light and darkness in the prologue to the Gospel of John, which is found in close association with the Word or *logos*. The Greek *logos* is found in Greek thinking contemporary with the New Testament, where it can mean an intermediate being between the heavenly and the earthly realms. But the opening words of John are "In the beginning"—echoing the opening words of Genesis. The first words spoken by the Creator in Genesis are "let there be light" (Gen. 1:3). John says that the *logos* not only was with God (which could apply to a demigod) but that he was God. Then John goes on to introduce the theme of the Word being the light which the darkness has not overcome. Darkness cannot mean the earth itself, for then the *logos* dwelling on earth and made flesh (Jn. 1:14) would have been overcome by the darkness. In Gnostic teaching, when the sparks were imprisoned in a body, the human spirit was overcome (drugged, or plunged in the sleep of unconsciousness). For Christians the light became an earth-dweller, while still remaining the God through whom heaven and earth were made.

It is always the use of a word or a sequence of words that determines the meaning. Hegelians and other spiritualists are accustomed to say that biblical words such as salvation, the Christ, the cross, and so on, are symbols. All words are symbols. The vital question is, What are they symbols *of*? When the Christ is made a symbol of the unity eternally present in the human consciousness aware of its divinity, then the biblical use of the term "Christ" has been left behind. When the cross is called the division between the past and the future, then this is Gnosticism and not Christian faith. The symbolism of the cross has been changed.

The same principle holds good in connection with the parallels I have been pointing out between the old and the new Gnosticism. Here different languages are involved, so naturally different words are being used. The point is that our experiences on earth are constant, whatever era we live in and whatever part of the globe we inhabit. The English word "liberation" means something more than the word freedom. It carries the special meaning connected with our experience of being set free in some particularly dramatic fashion. Two types of experience have this particular quality: being let out of prison, and being rescued by a friendly army when we have been living under an occupying army. A third type of experience is closely associated with these two, namely, being emancipated when we have been living as slaves. Every language possesses words that express these particular experiences. Old and new Gnostics see religious salvation exclusively in these terms. Christians see salvation through Jesus Christ as liberation solely as liberation from our imprisonment by sin or the occupation of our souls by sin. Yet even more prominently, salvation for Christians means cleansing through the blood of Christ and receiving the forgiveness enabling them to be reconciled to God.

When salvation is thought of as liberation only, then what we are being saved from can be nothing except our present condition as inhabitants of earth. As the Valentinian Formula puts it, liberation means knowing "whereinto we have been thrown." It means also knowing "whereto we speed"—which may be away from the finite into the infinite or away from the past and present into the future. Anywhere except the here and now! For Christians, however, this flight from the present is not salvation but further evidence of our sinful condition. Bunyan's Christian pilgrim speeds from the City of Destruction. Yet the pilgrim's flight is not from this earth, for it is upon this earth that he or she must make the Christian journey from this world to the world to come.

The Valentinian Formula requires Gnostics to know what birth is and what rebirth is. Gnostics know that birth is being thrown here into the prisonhouse of earth, and that rebirth is our awakening to awareness of being spirit-bearers. Christians believe that birth is God's good gift to his children. They celebrate with joy the birth of Jesus Christ because in Bethlehem the Word was made flesh. Yet the birth of any baby is also an occasion for celebration. Rebirth is being born again "through water and the Spirit" (Jn. 3:5). Knowledge that rebirth can take place is one of the heavenly things which *flesh* or the human consciousness cannot know except through God's revelation. But being born of the Spirit has nothing to do with being aware of having a spiritual nature that finds existence in the flesh an intolerable bondage.

The new Gnostics, of course, would deny that they repudiate existence in the flesh, since they execute an exodus from oppressive establishments precisely in order to build an earthly utopia. Yet, from a Christian perspective, first they have maligned birth and then they have misunderstood rebirth. "I tell you this, brethren: flesh and blood cannot inherit the kingdom of God, nor does the perishable inherit the imperishable"

(1 Cor. 15:50 RSV). The goodness of earth is real, but its goodness consists in the fact that it exists under the care of heaven without being heaven. Earth is God's good creation (though spoiled by human sin) and it has been created within limits because it is itself and not an emanation from God. As distinct from God, human glory lies in its limitations. The story of the Tower of Babel is told in the Bible to remind us of this truth. The great achievements of civilization come from respecting the limitations of earthly existence and using them to express concretely what is good about human life because it is finite. Shakespeare did not write about humanity in general. As an Englishman born into the Elizabethan Age, he wrote of the world he knew— and so was able to communicate with people of every age and country what it means to live on this earth. Van Gogh put a few ordinary sunflowers in a vase and so today people see what they had not seen before—the radiance of the ordinary caught by one individual's perception of what makes us all glad to be alive.

To fly from the past and the present in quest of an unlimited future is to try to build the Tower of Babel over again. It shows hatred of the concrete nature of God's good creation. If we say that the present is tolerable solely because of our hope for the future, we are seeing birth as Gnostics have always seen it and thinking of rebirth in a Gnostic fashion also. Only our hopes for a world different from the one into which we have been born keep us from despair. Only our faith in the deeds we can do to rid the earth of its limitations makes us devote our energies to effect *a permanent cultural revolution,* discovering a new way in which to be human. God has revealed to us what it means to be human through creating us male and female and setting us in the garden of earth to till it. He has also empowered us to name all the concrete, individual things the garden contains. This power, inherent in our ability to use language, is the source of all the human arts and sciences, opening to our understanding all the worlds of culture. When we say that we want to humanize man, then, what we are asking for is some other earth than the one God has given us in which to be stewards. We want to be reborn into a limitless world revealed to us by the spirit within us, a Gnostic pleroma which we imagine to be possible, because to the human spirit all things are possible.

The result of such imaginings is that we fly off into abstractions, leaving behind this earth and its limitations. Unlike Swift, we so love humanity that we forget John, Peter, and Thomas. As always happens when people forsake concrete actualities for abstract ideas, we may well end by killing John, Peter, and Thomas if we believe the permanent cultural revolution demands it.

So far, particular churches continue to show the kindly, humanitarian, liberal face of social gospel days when non-judgmental love was thought able to solve all human problems. Yet this is hardly the face of man today, when, so we are told, the contemporary consciousness is attuned to liberation and to social justice defined as absolute equality for all social groups. If it is not enough for us to be human beings because we need to be humanized, then clearly we shall have to be humanized forcibly whenever we will not submit willingly to the transformation. For those who resist moving in the direction to which world-history is moving must be wicked people. The politicized churches have aligned themselves with the forces of anti-liberalism by supporting violent liberation movements and also types of political action doing violence to the consciences of many citizens of the state. In the name of social justice, these Christians are saying that nobody has the right to impose any standard of morality whatsoever upon those who wish to behave as they choose; and the churches have most often spoken in support of a complete moral relativism because, they say, Christians must on no account seek to impose their beliefs on anyone.

In connection with one such issue of social justice, that of abortion, the Canadian philosopher George Grant has recently argued that today the old cultural liberalism has turned into a dogmatic belief in the triumph of the will. The modern view of the human will is that it is "the center of our aiming or seeking, the holding together of what we want." Dr. Grant takes his phrase "triumph of the will" from the title of Leni Riefenstahls' famous documentary of the thirties. *The Triumph of the Will* was a record of a convention of the National Socialist Party at

Nuremburg, and it has been called the most brilliant propaganda film of all time. Dr. Grant calls belief in the triumph of the will the essence of fascism. He is probably right. Yet I think the ideology to be older that the Nazis and older than Nietzsche, for it was clearly spelled out in *Goethe's* Faust. Moreover, like *Faust, The Triumph of the Will* showed obvious Gnostic overtones.

The film opens with an airplane, a speck in the sky, descending to earth and revealing itself to be the bearer of Adolf Hitler. The heavenly messenger has come from highest heaven to impart his secret *Gnosis.* He steps onto the earth, apparently a small, ordinary man. But his own people are awaiting him and they hail him as the liberator, the one whose words are not mere words but full of the energy of the celestial fire that can kindle the divine spark within his hearers and cause it to burst into flame. In Goethe's terminology, the Führer knows that in the beginning was not just the Word but the Deed. His words speak directly to the spirit of the German people and therefore cannot fail to make them burn with an equal energy, and cast off the enslaving chains binding them to their lower soul. This people is now ready to conquer the spirit that denies—in the present age embodied in the bourgeois capitalists and liberals, but above all in the Jews. For the subhuman Jews are the enemies of the pure spirit resident in the Aryan race, whose deeds prove them to be the agents of the world's destiny.

The will is indeed "the holding together of what we want," in the perspective of Goethe's *Faust.* For the deed proceeds from the operation of the higher soul that never rests in the present but always pushes on into the future. The triumph of the will, therefore, is the effective power of the creative energy flowing from the human spirit. It must be victorious, since its enemies are those weak souls clinging to the world of matter and the lower appetites.

Liberation thinkers are fond of saying that Christian words must cease to be used abstractly and become concrete. By this they mean that their abstract interpretations of Christian words such as salvation and sin must be applied to the present age, issuing in joining movements of liberation. In seeking to apply the abstract ideal of social justice, for example, the laws of a country (so they say) must be altered so that forward-looking people are not impeded in getting what they want. Dr. Grant, considering the question of abortion, notes that this principle means that whether or not abortion involves *killing* a fetus is irrelevant. The only thing that matters is whether people can treat their bodies as they desire. And, of course, getting rid of a fetus cannot be killing, because a fetus is living, but not a humanized, consciousness. It can only be viewed as a tissue of the body and *therefore* unimportant.

Again, we see that Gnostic thinking always comes back to contempt for the body, the concrete individual, and finally the earth itself. The triumph of the will is the triumph of abstract thinking. The wish to build the city of humanity by draining a swamp and placing the city over it is the desire to obliterate God's creation and "do our own thing!"

In part two of my study of the present state of Christian teaching in the life of mainline churches, I shall be looking at how traditional teachings can guide us back from abstractions to concrete ways of thinking that honor the earth as the place where God has set each of us to do his will and not our own. When being concrete has come to mean implementing our desires even when these endanger the fabric of society or even the continued existence of the earth, we need to be reminded that knowledge is not the same as wisdom and gaining what we believe to be our rights has no necessary connection with justice. Justice has little meaning where there is no understanding of righteousness in a nation.

Because ours is a fallen creation, the past can easily be read as the record of human wickedness, oppression, and greed. But it can be read also as the record of experience bringing wisdom—not inevitably growing wisdom, but wisdom again and again averting catastrophe. Traditional Christian teaching is no less fallible and marked by human sin than any other human tradition. Yet it has been guided by the belief that the gospel of Jesus Christ as contained in Scripture brings us the knowledge of who we are, where we have been placed, and where we are going because of the gift of redemption and rebirth; and the gospel shows us in whom we trust. The gospel is no Gnostic abstraction.

10. No Earthly Good: Epilogue to Part One

The conscience [the nature of man's inmost being] is . . . the place where God and the world meet. . . . worldly talk of God is godly talk of the world.

Gerhard Ebeling

The real danger is that liturgy creates a world of things over against the secular, instead of a vision of the sacredness of the secular.

Eric James

All generalizations have to admit the existence of a thousand exceptions. In the preceding chapters I have argued that the more the churches have decreased in numbers and in influence, the more they have departed from their traditional beliefs. As generalizations go, I think this one of mine is tolerably accurate.

My conclusion that the departure from traditional beliefs was largely motivated by the wish to capture lost prestige was prompted by the many statements made by church leaders and theologians to the effect that the most pressing need of the churches was to preach a message understandable by man today and adapted to mere contemporary needs. My contention that the churches *may* win more respect from an unbelieving world if they return to traditional Christian faith is a guess, one arising out of observation that people usually see an overeagerness to please as a sign of some failure of nerve. My plea that the churches should consider the traditional option for their own sakes and for the sake of the gospel is a confession of faith. Believing the Christian story as it has come to us down the ages to be true and the one means of our salvation, I grieve to see it rejected—especially for no very good reason. In part two of the present study, I shall try to show how there are many excellent reasons for considering the rejection of traditional Christianity both premature and tragic.

When spiritualists talk of Christians being called to meet the needs of the world, they claim to be speaking concretely. But the word "world," as they use it, does not mean our earth and the people living there. It means the human communities built by sinful people, the fallen world, the world Christians are not to love, "because nothing the world has to offer . . . could ever come from the Father" (1 Jn. 2:16 JB). This world is not a unity, for it is actually a conglomeration of many worlds: the world of politics; the world of culture; the world of economics; the world of fashion; the world of religion; the world of speculative thought. Apart from these specific worlds the world is really an abstraction. In the Bible, all these worlds are lumped together because they all have one thing in common—the fact that they are all built on self-will and seldom recognize that human beings have been created to obey the will of God. So, when any new agenda for the churches is drawn up for the purpose of serving the world, Christians are being asked to put themselves at the disposal of the world's will. They are to help human societies organize themselves to get what their members want, whether or not it is what they need, and whether or not it is just and good.

Traditional Christian faith understands heaven and earth to be two existing realities. God exists because he *is* everlasting. Earth and its inhabitants exist because God created them. But post-Enlightenment thinking in the various forms found today imagines only one reality—spirit. When we see it rightly, matter is (in A. N. Whitehead's phrase) "barely to be distinguished from non-entity." And this is simply the old Gnostics' view of life in the body as a drunken sleep from which we need to be awakened or as a sinking down into a bottomless morass where the spirit drowns. These images of earthly life are certainly not consciously present in the imaginations of our contemporaries. Yet we have only to notice the images that they do use to see how the gnostic themes persist. "I've got to find out who I really am—discover my real identity." "Be yourself—dare to dream and believe in your dreams—march to the beat of a different drum." "Don't be tied down by the past—live for the future." "The human dawn will break if we really believe in it." All these images imply consciousness of the Gnostic unknown God (the *alien* God because he has nothing in common with life in the body) causing dreams of the kingdom of light to break into the darkness of earth and bringing the human spirit to awareness of its own real nature.

The statements at the head of this chapter show a continental and a British theologian urging us to make our talk about God relevant to the world. When the American theologian Harvey Cox comments on the statement by Ebeling, he refers to "an event in which man and the world are seen for what they really are." He concludes that what Ebeling calls "godly talk of the world" and *vice versa* is what he himself calls talking of God politically. All this looks somewhat confusing. But the confusion has come about simply because these theologians have not declared their myths.

The three theologians all are drawing upon the Gnostic myth of there being only one reality—spirit. Existence upon earth is not a real form of life, because spirit alone gives life. The One True Reality has two aspects, a higher and a lower. Higher reality is the unknown God (unknown to mere earth dwellers) and his kingdom of light. Lower reality is the human spirit and the world which the human spirit creates through its self-consciousness. Thus, when we talk about "the world," we are referring to the spiritual creations located upon earth, but not belonging to it. And, when we speak of God and the world, or of the sacred and the secular, we are speaking of the higher and the lower aspects of the one reality.

Seeing man and the world as they really are, therefore, is seeing them as spiritual realities. Today, some Christians have outgrown the biblical view of two realities and do not believe in "another world" or the heavenly kingdom where God rules. When they pray, "Thy kingdom come, thy will be done on earth as it is in heaven," they have to translate the prayer into the one reality form, its true meaning. The prayer now reads:

> May we always discern the higher reality in the lower: God in the world; the sacred in the secular. May the human spirit always remember its identity with God the Supreme Spirit and so fashion its world that a vision of the sacredness of the secular shines brightly. May we always remember that the religions of the world are ordained to give us ever-increasing God-consciousness; so at last religion as a separate human "world" will wither away and all become sacred because the sacred is wholly one with the secular.

Harvey Cox wrote *The Secular City* (1965) to show how Christians in the modern age had reached the point in the upward march of religious consciousness when they no longer needed to believe in a sacred reality existing on its own. So now they could worship God by serving the new secular world and its culture. Cox used a politico-military image to explain his belief in religion now being no longer the way in which man today became conscious of God. Instead, "the revolutionary regime has seized power but the symbols of authority are still in the hands of the old displaced rulers." In the religious world this meant that people were still being told they must worship God in the churches instead of worshipping by joining in revolutionizing the conditions of modern urban life. In the secular world it meant "that man is invited to make the whole universe over into a human place."

Abstract phrases about man humanizing the universe have no actual relation to anything taking place here on the earth. Men and women are living and dying as they always have

91

done; finding this earth to be a place of many joys and many sorrows; hoping for some improvement in their lot and working to remove some obstacles to what they believe will be a better life. When they achieve one goal, they may find some satisfaction or they may find nothing but disappointment. In fact, no one can possibly say whether or not we are better off than any of our ancestors. Few of us would wish to return to a previous age—and why should we, since this is the one we know and life in any age is uniquely fascinating? Yet we know very well that our gains in mastery over nature and our ability today to prolong life and make it more comfortable and less laborious have brought with them great losses as well. It is perfectly possible to argue (as some contemporary writers have done) that, in terms of stress, insecurity, fear, hopelessness, and exposure to torture or violent death, ours is the least enviable age since recorded history began. But we do not have to hold extreme views, one way or the other, to understand very well that all claims for the present age as the dawning of a new vision of an earthly utopia just over the horizon are manifestly false.

No, the old Gnostic faith in one reality is of no earthly good. It is especially *un*earthly in its modern progressivist forms. Christian tradition teaches belief in another and a better world than this one. But it does not write off the earth and leave it to the devil and his angels. All creation is to benefit from the salvation brought through the cross of Jesus Christ. Meanwhile, Christian hope does not absorb Christian faith into itself, holding out grandiose visions of a perfected future for humanity while leaving individual men and women to sacrifice themselves for a mirage. For each and every one of us Christian faith has a message for the journey we must make upon this earth, every step of which is one teaching us to wonder anew at the marvelous and concrete joys contained in God's creation.

TWO   **THE PRODIGALS'
RETURN: RECOVERING
THE CHRISTIAN
TRADITION**

11. Friends of the Earth

The Lord God took the man and put him in the garden of Eden to till it and keep it.

Genesis 2:15 RSV

"That is well said," replied Candide, "but we must cultivate our garden."

From *Candide* (1759) by Voltaire

Francois Marie Arouet de Voltaire would have been vastly amused to see one of his own sentences paired with a verse from the Bible, a book he considered a collection of superstitions. In his day the most famous man in Europe, Voltaire is often thought to be the embodiment of the spirit of the Enlightenment. But all the brave bulls do not come from one herd, and Christians can learn much from the skeptical "laughing philosopher."

Candide was inspired by an event and a dogma. The event was the great Lisbon earthquake of 1755, a catastrophe causing many to doubt the goodness of God. The dogma was the declaration by the philosopher Liebniz that, since God was perfect he had created a world as perfect as any world could possibly be. Voltaire's story is about the simpleminded Candide, who accepts without question the assurance of his tutor Doctor Pangloss that

95

ours is the best of all possible worlds. After suffering one disaster after another, including the Lisbon earthquake (which actually saves his life), Candide is able to rescue all his friends from death or slavery because of his practical common sense. He buys a small farm and decides to settle down and forget about trying to solve the mystery of the meaning of the universe.

Voltaire encouraged his contemporaries to adopt the yardstick of *good sense* to measure teachings about human ideals, using laughter to discredit speculative systems of thought claiming to have discovered the nature of ultimate reality. In the next century, the Danish writer Søren Kierkegaard made it his life's work to defend traditional Christian faith against the system builders of his era. His principal target was the philosophy of Hegel, then being warmly received by the progressive leaders of the national Lutheran Church in Denmark. Acknowledged today as his country's greatest literary stylist, and also one of the outstanding thinkers of all time, Kierkegaard used the same kind of wit to advocate Christianity that Voltaire had used to attack it. But whereas Voltaire had been content simply to mock the pretensions of abstract thinking, Kierkegaard brought his wide knowledge of philosophy to bear upon contemporary myths, dissecting them with skill.

Kierkegaard said that his mission was "to introduce Christianity into Christendom." The teachings of the New Testament had long been overlaid by the values of Western culture; and now, with the acceptance by the churches of Hegel's pseudo-religion of absolute spirit, they were in danger of being lost entirely. Those calling themselves Christians (and, in contemporary Denmark, that was everybody) had to learn all over again what being a Christian meant. In a torrent of writings appearing rapidly one after another during the 1840s, Kierkegaard tried to open minds that had been closed by Hegelian abstractions. His method was what he called "indirect communication." Not until his *Training in Christianity* (1850) did he advocate the classic Christian doctrines by name. In this book he explained, like Wesley before him, that no Christianity was genuine which did not start with the doctrine of Original Sin.

Kierkegaard was the first to realize that the central feature of system building was its abstract nature. The concrete, realistic language of the Bible was turned by speculative thinkers into bookless abstractions. People were forgetting that they were human beings living on this earth when they accepted Hegel's theories of world history, imagining instead that they were able "to think God's thought after him" (as Hegelians claimed to do), because they participated in universal humanity. The new philosopher, Kierkegaard said, thought he understood the world process from beginning to end. Yet as he is explaining his infinite knowledge, he does not know that in the next few seconds he will have to stop orating and blow his nose.

Exponents of philosophical Idealism (whom I have called spiritualists) held that there was only one reality, the realm accessible to thought. Attacking Hegel's absolute Idealism, Kierkegaard called it *absentminded*. It had forgotten the evident fact that we exist as limited beings living in time and space. God has created this earth and put us in it. Eternity is not our birthright because we possess spirit. Eternal life is a gift which God bestows upon us through his grace and in spite of our sin. Christianity, he explained, can be thought of as an education— but not an education making us clever enough and energetic enough to turn this earth into a utopia. No! By means of this education we learn to immerse ourselves ever more deeply into existence! We are all born as individual human beings, but to live as individuals taking responsibility for our actions is something we learn only slowly and painfully. Pride in possessing self-consciousness has to give way to self-understanding. Self-understanding is knowing the place where God has set us and what he expects us to do there. It is not to believe the promise of the serpent in Eden, "You shall be as gods" (Gen. 3:5), a promise which Hegel had said to be confirmed by God's own Word. It is to know we are mortal, with the possibility to become the children of God through faith.

So, for Kierekgaard, the Christian category of thinking is *the individual,* as opposed to the Hegelian category of *humanity.* Concreteness here replaces abstraction, and gratitude for finite existence replaces the wish to escape from the finite into the infinite Whole. In place of Hegel's dialectic of thesis, antithesis, and synthesis that claimed to show the entire meaning of world history and its inevitable progress towards final perfection, Kierkegaard put what he called the dialectic of Either/Or. This dialectic was the result of the Christian belief that we know nothing about the universe as a process unfolding in stages of increasing perfection. All we know is the present where we are confronted by the necessity of making choices. At any one moment, in fact, we have only a choice between two courses of action. Either we do something or we do not. (For instance, *either* we blow our nose now, *or* we wait until later to do it. Afterwards, the need for blowing it may have gone *or* we are not able to put it off any longer.) For Christians, said Kierkegaard, the all-inclusive either/or is the choice between accepting the gospel message or refusing it. We shall continue to meet other either/ors all our lives, but the crucial choice has been made.

Kierkegaard's *no* to culture Christianity in its Hegelian form has been the model for nearly all twentieth-century Christian thinkers who have resisted the flight from traditional Christianity evident ever since the age of Enlightenment. The most influential of these thinkers earlier in our century was the Swiss theologian Karl Barth. Educated in Germany under liberal Christian teachers, including Adolf Harnack (an eminent disciple of Ritschl's school), Barth's *no* to liberalism in theology came after World War I, when he found that his teachers were eagerly supporting the German cause as the *Christian* cause. Harnack actually wrote some of the Kaiser's speeches for him. Reading Kierkegaard was one of the chief reasons why Barth challenged the current teachings of the churches in the way he did. The churches, said Barth, had emerged from the nineteenth century *religionistic, anthropocentric,* and *humanistic.* Following the indictment Martin Luther had brought against the Roman Church in the sixteenth century, Barth said that the liberal churches would not let God be God. He declared, "You cannot speak about God by speaking about man in a loud voice." Here he was protesting against the human spirit being considered the finite form of the infinite or Absolute Spirit.

One of Barth's early books was a collection of essays entitled *The Word of God and the Word of Man* (ET 1928). The English title stressed Barth's contention that the two should never be confused. Indeed, he constructed his whole theology at this time upon the belief that the Word of God always comes to us in the form of a *yes* and a *no*. (The influence of Kierkegaard's either/or is obvious. Our choosing to follow one path or the other when we make decisions depends upon whether we take the path which God commands.) God has said *yes* to us by sending Jesus Christ to earth for our salvation. Our human *no* of unbelief cannot frustrate God's gracious purpose for his children, but it can mean that we exclude ourselves from his promises to us. God's *no* is seen in the limits he has set to our actions by placing us within the created world. We can never overstep these limits, claiming that the human spirit can be raised to divine humanity. And the notion that we can build the kingdom upon earth or humanize the earth is patently absurd.

Both Kierkegaard and Barth showed that, while Christians are "not of the world" because "friendship with the world is enmity with God" (Jas. 4:4 RSV), they can be friends of the earth. The Danish and the Swiss Christian thinkers were steeped in European culture and eagerly sought out pleasure in the arts. Kierkegaard was a brilliant critic of the theater. Barth found constant relaxation in listening to the music of Mozart. A theologian might be expected to prefer J. S. Bach, with his solid Lutheran faith finding expression in his majestic oratorios. Barth preferred Mozart, a nominal Catholic whose only religion was Freemasonry. The point is that Christians love human productions precisely because they are of this world and not religious. (Of course, this would not prevent them loving Bach's music, since nonchristians also love it unreservedly.) Kierkegaard praised his countryman Hans Christian Andersen for his story-telling, but earned the author's enmity by criticizing his efforts to become a *serious* writer.

Spiritualists claim to catch a vision of the sacredness of the secular. This claim is always, in Barth's terminology, one ignoring God's *no*. It is the attempt to overstep the limits God has set. It is a denial of the original goodness of creation. It proclaims an attitude of enmity towards the earth. Godly talk of the world and worldly talk of God are both equal absurdities. When people love God and are friends of the earth, they talk of God as the Bible talks of him—in godly fear. For they know that all human speech *about* God soon becomes either trivial or blasphemous. The only genuine way of approaching God in human words is the way of prayer or talking *to* God. And when people love the earth as God's good creation, then they keep to the worldly way of speaking about it. Christians, if they are wise, know very well that their understanding of creation as coming from God does not necessarily make them better at speaking about it than atheists and skeptics. In fact, they may be put to shame by the latter, whose appreciation of the earth is often wider and deeper than their own.

Human arts and sciences are good in themselves, and not because they reflect some spiritual or religious capacity in human nature. They reflect simply the capacity to love the earth. This love may issue in wishing to look at the earth in order to learn more about it—the way of the natural sciences; or to examine exactly how human beings living on earth behave individually and collectively—the way of the social sciences; or to express how human consciousness reacts to the whole experience of living in the earth—the way of literature and the arts. In the last instances, however, we should notice very carefully that no writer, artist, or musician ever tried to deal abstractly with *the whole experience*. These practitioners always deal concretely with one precise area of experience known here and now. Proust based his many volumes of *Remembrance of Things Past* on his sensations when dipping a piece of cake into a cup. T. S. Eliot wrote his *Four Quartets* after listening constantly to the last string quartets of Beethoven. Picasso painted his *Guernica* after hearing the accounts of the bombing of that city during the Spanish Civil War. Artists start with one immediate stimulus making them wish to give this moment a permanent form, and then they continue to weave a tapestry around the moment that contains a lifetime of experiences.

Have we come a long way from the subject of traditional Christian teaching? No! Because it is particularly in the human arts that the true *worldly* way of looking at the things of earth can be seen. And the Christian view of life requires a clear separation of the sacred from the secular. Christianity has nothing to fear from the secular experience. In fact, when Christians condemn the secular life they are telling God he has made a mistake. He should have created us without bodies and put us in his heavenly kingdom rather than imprisoning us, even for a short time, in the hell of time and space.

The only enemy of Christian faith is some other faith, one of these being *secularism*. Secularism is a religious interpretation of human life dogmatically ruling out God and his kingdom and believing that human life is an ultimate reality. If we look at philosophy and the arts down the ages we see at once that secularism, when it is consistent, is wholly pessimistic. The reason for this is fairly obvious.

All things on earth decay and die. The universe itself must die, or else it must repeat itself in an endless cycle of births and deaths. Thus all human life goes down to death and to nothingness. Secularism can become optimistic solely when it takes into itself (most often without saying so) a religious concept of salvation or way of overcoming nothingness. The Gnostic view of salvation being one of the very old forms of explaining religious salvation, it is quite natural that it should have been revived in our own day. We live in an increasingly secularized culture, one not much given to philosophy or any strenuous thinking. Our culture used to be Christian. So, just as in the second century, the Gnostic view of salvation has been grafted onto the Christian one with the result considered much more up-to-date and "scientific."

Secularism is so discouraging a creed that nearly everyone always prefers to give it a religious twist to make it seem attractive. But there are always one or two bold souls with the courage to face the logic of its premises. Voltaire was one. In our own

101

century, Bertrand Russell was another. Saying, "I believe that when I die I shall rot," Russell saw that the universe also was headed for death; and he laughed at the dogma of inevitable progress. Yet, like Voltaire, he knew that people of goodwill ought to be active in doing what was possible to make life more tolerable for their contemporaries.

There is a superficial resemblance between the attitudes summed up in, "Let us eat and drink, for tomorrow we die" (1 Cor. 15:32 RSV) and, "As long as we have food and clothing, let us be content with that" (1 Tim. 6:8 JB). Yet the second is Christian, while the first is hedonistic. Hedonism is secularism wearing blinders and refusing to face up to the finality of death. The brave or stoic secularist is very near to the Christian in believing that we must live one day at a time and be grateful for each day's mercies. Perhaps it was not accidental that Bertrand Russell's daughter became a Christian missionary. Secularists without hope but also without illusions do not necessarily become cynics. They too may become friends of the earth.

Religious people all too often are afflicted with a deadly seriousness. That is why they feel they have to denounce everybody who does not agree with them and show such a lack of love. Today, theologians of hope and liberation reveal and surpass any inquisitor of the fifteenth and sixteenth centuries in the savage ferocity of their rooting out of the true faith any unbelievers. But secularists of the stamp of Voltaire and Russell love to laugh. Not expecting any permanent improvement in the world, they can afford to forgive others for not being perfect.

Refusing to be religious, Voltaire said we should cultivate our garden. The biblical view of human existence is that God intended us to do just that. He wanted us to be secular men and women who also know that the right way of living a secular life is in the service of the eternal God. Any other way leads to death. In the history of God's people, as the Bible tells it, trouble came when the people became religious instead of obeying the living Lord. The people went after strange gods and forgot the one who had supported them through all their journeys upon earth. It is no different today.

Secular people laugh and cry, for that is the human way. When they try to ignore death, their laughter is hollow and their tears are bitter. Those who are prepared to face the finality of death find that nothing in daily life is so supremely serious that they cannot find a joke in it, while nothing is so trivial that they cannot see in it a reason for tears. Christians also laugh and cry while they live in this *saeculum* or present age. Kierkegaard's funny little tales that punctuate his philosophical arguments and Barth's jests are essential products of their Christian faith as much as are their laments over their fellow Christians who have lost touch with the faith that alone can support them on their earthly journey.

But for Christians it is not death that is the wholly serious thing—although it *is* serious. The only truly serious matters are God's care for us and our sinful disobedience to his will. Therefore, God's revelation of himself in Jesus Christ is beyond laughter and tears. It calls forth wondering awe.

Since the faith once and for all delivered to the saints is the means of our salvation, interpreting this faith for our generation is also serious. Yet here especially we have to remember that we are human. *Our* statements concerning the nature of the Christian faith—however traditional and orthodox they may be—are not the final word. Theologians in their own way are cultivating their garden although they know that this is not their own garden but the Lord's. They must not take themselves too seriously, either. Their words must always carry this confession: "we are merely servants: we have done no more than our duty" (Lk. 17:10 JB). In this chapter I have reviewed the contribution made by Kierkegaard and Barth to the Christian understanding of what it means to live on the earth created by God to be our place of existence. The next chapter looks especially at Dietrich Bonhoeffer, who made it his especial concern to grapple with the meaning of the secular.

12. The Lord of the Earth

The earth is the Lord's and the fulness thereof, the world and those who dwell therein.

Psalm 24:1 RSV

God does not give us everything we want, but he does fulfil his promises, i.e., he remains Lord of the earth, he preserves his Church, constantly renewing our faith and not laying on us more than we can bear, gladdening us with his nearness and help, hearing our prayers, and leading us along the best and straightest path to himself. By his faithfulness in doing this, God creates in us praise for himself.

Dietrich Bonhoeffer

The gospel does not need to be brought up-to-date. That would mean simply making it conform to cultural norms and so making it prisoner of the prejudices of a particular era. Yet in every generation some aspects of the gospel more urgently need to be brought to people's attention. Kierkegaard emphasized how each individual must answer the call of faith, because Hegelian Christians were thinking of humanity in the abstract. Barth emphasized God's commands, his *yes* and *no* to us, because liberal Christians were thinking that we had to bring in God's kingdom ourselves. By the 1930s another situation had arisen.

104

Barth's teachings about the Word of God influenced many European Christians in the years between the world wars, though they never struck deep roots in Britain and America. One of Barth's loyal but critical disciples was Dietrich Bonhoeffer. Today he is best remembered for his death at the hands of the Gestapo for involvement in the abortive attempt to take Hitler's life, and also for the (much misunderstood) *Letters and Papers from Prison* (ET 1953). Accepting Barth's stand upon the authority of God's Word, Bonhoeffer concentrated upon how we best could obey God's Word in a secular culture that had forgotten God. His book *The Cost of Discipleship* (ET 1948) shows this emphasis.

Bonhoeffer's understanding of secular Christianity was based on his reading of Martin Luther's call to his contemporaries to live their faith in their secular callings instead of thinking a religious calling (monastic life) to be the higher way of following Christ. Barth was a Reformed or Calvinistic churchman. Bonhoeffer was a traditional German Lutheran, so Luther was his hero.

Bonhoeffer said that we must be Christians "in the world." There were two ways of avoiding Christ's call to discipleship. One was the way taken by fearful, weak Christians. They tried to save their own souls, leaving the earth to the devil. The other path was taken by the strong and energetic Christians. These people had "a thousand plans" for improving the world. Seemingly going in opposite directions, the two paths came from the same point: hatred of God's creation. One set of Christians thought God cared only for what was spiritual and therefore asked his children to fly to heaven. The other set thought in exactly the same way, except they imagined God's children were meant to show their "spirited" action here on earth. Against both these misinterpretations of the gospel call, Bonhoeffer insisted that Christians certainly should prepare themselves for heaven. But here on earth they had a secular calling to follow. They were not to pride themselves on the religious quality of their actions. Rather they should be good citizens and do what they could to make their society better, without confusing their good works with advancing the kingdom. The kingdom, insofar as it is seen on earth, is present in the church, the communion of saints. And God himself builds up his church, not human efforts.

Thus Bonhoeffer carried on Barth's teaching that creation was God's *no* to human pretensions to "be as gods" and do God's work for him. Bonhoeffer also knew Kierkegaard's writings well. He expressed his belief that Christians should live as secular people in the world, the Kierkegaardian teaching that faith requires Christians to immerse themselves in existence. God is Lord of the earth, said Bonhoeffer; and if we are to be the children of God, we must first know ourselves to be children of the earth. He totally rejected the cult of the human. Yet he pointed out that secular humanists are frequently much more admirable individuals than the Christians we meet. They have "come of age" in the sense in which thinkers of the Enlightenment spoke of leaving a state of tutelage. They know that they do not need *religion* to make sense of the universe or to behave altruistically rather than selfishly. Christians too should come of age in this sense. They should not ask people to adopt the Christian religion in order to be good and happy. They should not pray to God to do things for them which they could easily do for themselves. God is not to be used but to be served. His kingdom is not what we want, or think we want. It is to be entered and is entered when we join the church of Jesus Christ.

The words of Bonhoeffer at the head of this chapter are from the *Letters and Papers from Prison*. Writing to his friend Eberhard Bethge from his Berlin prison during the summer of 1944, Bonhoeffer said that two scriptural verses had been much in his mind: "And the Lord said to Moses, 'Is the Lord's hand shortened? Now you shall see whether my word will come true for you or not'" (Num. 11:23 RSV); and "For all the promises of God find their Yes in him [Christ]; and that is why we utter the Amen through him, to the glory of God" (2 Cor. 1:20 RSV). And then he wrote the passage I have quoted. For Bonhoeffer in wartime Germany, hope did not lie in the future, in the eventual overthrow of the terrible oppression of the Nazi regime (which he had tried to hasten and failed), or in any vision of liberation—he knew nothing awaited him but death. His secular Christianity meant doing what he could do here on earth, upheld by the knowledge that God remains Lord of the earth. When he was finally led out for execution, his last words were, "This is the end—for me the beginning of life."

Bonhoeffer's secular Christian outlook may well be contrasted with a Gnostic outlook, old and new. For the old Gnostics, the dark God ruled this earth, except for the sparks of light he had imprisoned. There his hand was shortened. He could not win the war against spirit. For new Gnostics, only human spirituality properly oriented through hope in the future wins the war against oppression. Old Gnostics imagined the cosmic warfare to be between paired opposites: light/dark; spirit/matter; ascending spirits/the aeons. New Gnostics also think in terms of paired opposites: new/old; future/past; liberation/oppression. Old and new Gnostics explain the pairs as cosmic powers eternally warring. Yet on the earth our experience of the pairs is that they belong together even though they are opposites.

We live our lives among things both old and new. Some old things we preserve with the utmost care; others we discard because the new are needed as the old wear out. Sometimes *new* is not as good as *old;* and sometimes *new* is much better. Similarly, living between the past and the future, we have to think of both. The past is immeasurably the more important. When we forget the past, we have no identity because we have no history and nothing to make us persons. The future is something we need to consider, since tomorrow is an extension of today. If we make no plans for the future we are foolish. On the other hand, if we plan for the future without any idea that every single one of our plans may easily miscarrry, we are more foolish still. "Fool!" was what God said to the futurist in the parable of Jesus (Lk. 12:20). As for liberation/oppression, our oppression by the weight of the air is what liberates us to move around on the earth. We remain reasonably free from oppression by others when we are not liberated from the rule of law. But the two

107

terms are always relative. The medieval serf and the poor urban worker can be seen in many ways on the liberation/oppression scale. In some ways the serf was less free than his modern counterpart, in other ways more free. When the serfs were liberated, they entered a different state of oppression. So it is always. When Hitler liberated Austria in 1938, he was cheered as the Great Liberator. But Jews, republicans, and anti-Nazis did not cheer; and many champions of the greater Germany later regretted having cheered.

Light/darkness is perhaps the archetype of all paired opposites. In all the cultures we know, good and evil are so identified. We think of the coming of the dawn as liberation from the oppression of darkness. At the same time, the coming of night also descends as a benediction upon tired souls. On earth, unceasing light would be hell. In his novel *1984*, George Orwell used this fact to effect. His hero thinks of a man he has met as the one who will liberate the country from totalitarian oppression. He writes in his diary, "We shall meet in a place where there is no darkness." The hero finds the meeting place is the headquarters of the Ministry of Love, where the glare of artificial light in the prison cells is never dimmed. And his liberator is a head of the Thought Police.

The light/darkness image covers a wide spectrum of experience. So *white* is good, *black* is evil. The expression, "black is beautiful," has then to be invented to counter the theory of white supremacy—although whites are anything but white in color, nor are blacks black. Death is *going down into the dark.* Knowing sorrow is *a period of darkness.* Gaining knowledge or having an inspiration is *seeing the light.* For Bible readers, however, God creates light first of all. But then he goes on to create day and night, each being equally his good creation. Light does not necessarily war with darkness.

Gnostics of all types take the paired opposites abstractly and then apply them literally to the things of earth. Considering the scorn which self-styled enlightened minds have always heaped upon biblical literalists, their own literalism is surprising but undeniable. They literally believe that the past fights against the future and oppression against liberation. Over the question of matter *versus* spirit they are more reticent, as they are over the creator God *versus* the highest spirit. Their language betrays them, all the same. Humanity, humanization, man today, contemporary consciousness—all these and related concepts speak of abstractions applied literally in order to elevate spirit and downgrade matter. And process theologians make no secret of their conviction that our physical universe must give way to a spiritual one.

On earth, we have no experience of the human spirit except as an individual consciousness within a body. Humanity does not inhabit the earth, men and women do. The possibility of entering into personal relationships presupposed separate individuals *not* gathered into a mass by Teilhardian *unanimisation*. Teilhard de Chardin, indeed, protests that his myth of an evolution to a spiritual omega point enhances rather than banishes personality. In the new world into which we "are being born," he says, each "thinking unit" will "only act (if he agrees to act) in the consciousness, become natural and instinctive to all, of furthering a work of total personalization." What could be fairer than that? Only here nothing is personal! Persons are not being born (except when childbirth is going on), for they are either born or not. Persons are not thinking units, for they are uniquely themselves. When consciousness has become natural and instinctive, choice is ruled out. Besides, what would happen if a single unit did not agree to continue producing inedible honey called total personalization in the cosmic beehive? The rest of the units would turn on it and naturally and instinctively destroy it.

Persons cannot be put in a box labeled "total personalization." Even the productions of persons cannot be handled like that. All the novels ever written would not add up to an entity called total fictionalization. We can use abstract words when they are convenient, saying maybe that Shakespeare, Newton, Lincoln, Cézanne, Grieg, and George Washington Carver have enriched humanity. This is no more than to say that a host of individual people have found their personal lives made richer because such persons have existed. All words can be employed

109

so as to honor the Lord of the earth by appreciating the companions he has given us to share our earthly journey. But we do him little honor when we call these companions thinking units. God told Moses to lead the people of Israel out of bondage in Egypt. But then, that was before we were being born into a new age when thinking units were to be his agents and total personalization the promised land.

Honoring and serving the Lord of the earth means turning to what Bonhoeffer called "the nearest thing at hand." Our neighbor is always nearest us, and that is why the biblical great commandment makes love of neighbor its second part, following love of God. Our neighbor is no mere unit in total humanity, but always possesses a face and a name. Swift understood this before Kierkegaard and Bonhoeffer put it forward as a central theme of the Christian faith. The Bible is a book full of names, and down the centuries it was never doubted that Christianity was a faith passed on from person to person within the community of the church. At least, it was never doubted until the nineteenth-century spiritualists came along. Earlier, of course, the Deists had tried to turn Christianity into an impersonal religion of timeless truths. But Deism had remained a religion for intellectuals. While the spirit of Deism had infiltrated the churches in the eighteenth century, it was always regarded as a religion outside the Christian tradition. When Bonhoeffer advocated a secular Christianity he was trying to restore a broken tradition, bringing once again to people's attention the concrete nature of Christian love. Loving God meant loving individuals created by God to be individuals. Indeed, it meant loving all of God's creation made up of actual persons, places, and things—each unique in itself.

Gnostic hatred of the creation and of the God who made it issued in two ways of looking at the universe, two distinct yet interconnected aspects of *gnosis*. These two forms of the Gnostic myth are alive in our own time, the first in process theologies and the second in theologies of liberation and hope and in political theology. Bonhoeffer knew only different kinds of liberal Christianity, in which the Gnostic elements were less pronounced than in later radical Christianity of the years following

110

World War II. He called these theologies *philosophies of religion*, not giving them the status of being Christian theologies. They had nothing to do with the promises of God in Jesus Christ. Bonhoeffer's insistence that Christian faith had nothing to do with religion was crucial for him. It is most helpful for us today, because it explains how a full-fledged Gnosticism has been able to captivate some churches.

Of the two Gnostic ways of looking at the universe, the first was the contemplative way. Gnostics contemplated world history from the standpoint of eternity. What they saw there was an advancing process. Light was progressively entering the darkness of this earth. While most Christian Gnostics identified the arrival of the heavenly messenger with the appearance of Jesus upon the earth, they did not think that no light had ever entered the earth from the highest heaven before. Some Gnostics taught that the messenger had arrived soon after the demiurge had formed his prison house, appearing time after time in various incarnations, and only finally appearing as Jesus. This view of a continuing revelation of the light is identical to that of the many mediators advanced by Schleiermacher, except that Schleiermacher did not talk about the founders of religions being reincarnations of the same messenger.

If heavenly light appearing on earth was an ongoing process, there was no reason why Jesus should be the final form of the messenger. Mani, a third-century Persian, claimed to be the Holy Spirit promised by Jesus and thus to possess a *gnosis* more complete than the one Jesus had taught. Manichaeism spread rapidly, and soon became the chief rival to Christianity. Augustine of Hippo, the great father of the Western church, was for ten years a Manichaean.

Process theologies are the heirs of the contemplative or speculative side of Gnostic teaching. This explains why Christian process thinkers are so insistent upon saying that we are now entering a new stage in the process of creation, why a new generation of humanized thinking units is *being born*. Jesus is certainly the original Redeemer of human spirituality; but, while the spirit of Jesus still saves man today, some new revela-

111

tion wholly contemporary in form is required. Teilhard de Chardin actually speaks of his theory of the universe evolving towards the omega-point of pure spirituality as *a new revelation.* Hegel believed that his philosophy of absolute spirit becoming self-conscious in humanity was a final unveiling of the whole truth about the universe. No further revelation was required.

When Marx turned the Hegelian philosophy "right-way up," he said, "Hitherto philosophers have explained the world. Our task is to change it." Marx's words are a good introduction to the second way in which Gnostics looked at the universe and the place of humanity in it.

In the contemplative Gnostic view, all is for the best in this world. We have only to wait until finally there will be no more matter, no more earthly prisonhouse, no more demiurge—for heavenly light *must* finally shine forth as the one reality and all shadows fall before it. The evil demiurge and his angels are themselves simply shadows cast by the light that falls on matter; and, by its very nature, matter is transient. True, we may have to wait a few millennia until all darkness fades away. We spirits are eternal—so why be impatient? But other Gnostics were in a hurry. Their argument was this: "There is a war going on between the powers of light and darkness. Certainly, light is destined to win and its victory cannot be hastened, since all is decreed beforehand by the all-sufficient light. But we must declare ourselves to be on the side of light, exercise the freedom which is the recognition of necessity, and fight the wicked agents of darkness."

We can see, then, why the writings of the process theologians are all sweetness and encouragement; why they preach optimism and even (as Teilhard does) say that the threat of atomic destruction is the best guarantee of the unification of humanity and of complete humanization in the distant future. They take the first Gnostic way. Liberation theologians and their kin, on the other hand, are all energetically on fire, demanding action *now.* We must execute an immediate exodus from all oppressive establishments; we must join liberation movements; and, especially, we must practice the denunciation of all oppressors and also root out all traces of the oppressive consciousness from ourselves. They take the second Gnostic way.

Bonhoeffer's advice to Christians was not to be religious but to be secular disciples of Christ, to "stay close to the earth." Both the contemplative and the energetic Gnostics will not tolerate that. Their "smooth, decent words" (to use Wesley's phrase) and their shrill words condemning all who oppose their views are alike spoken to call people away from thinking God's creation to be good. Only creativity is good. The world process is not yet good, but it is becoming better, and eventually it will be perfect. So say the contemplatives. Only creativity is good, and creativity is found within self-conscious humanity and *therefore* within those of us who are energetically fighting the powers of oppression. So say the activists, the world changers. Neither the contemplatives nor the activists spare any of their time on a God who is Lord of the earth and preserves his church. The only God they want is an evolving God who lives in the contemporary consciousness and makes his church move with the times and concentrate upon humanizing the world.

In the Bible there are many images of God's providential care, a personal care cosmic in its range, a care that continues with us into the unknown future and brings us at last to the heavenly city. In the Bible there are also images of the Christian life as a life of warfare, of a never-ending struggle against the powers of darkness. For both, walking in security, protected by a Good Shepherd, and having to struggle to overcome sin and the effects of sin are experiences we have as we make our earthly progress. Yet the biblical images are always concrete and utterly different from the Gnostic vision of spirit on its way to banish matter and obliterate earthly existence.

Christians who stay close to the earth and to the Lord of the earth, as Bonhoeffer believed they must in order to be true to biblical faith, will shun both Gnostic paths to salvation. Instead of thinking that abstractions inside their heads actually exist or will exist here on earth, they will thank their Creator for the concretely complex diversity of the created world. Instead of dismissing what is past, they will respect traditions

113

without worshipping them, recognizing they are human ways of preserving what our wise ancestors considered worth preserving. Instead of wishing to make the present serve the future, they will take each day as it comes as a gift unlike the previous day, yet like it in passing from hopeful morning to weary evening. Instead of raging against the oppressive consciousness, they will try to lessen the burdens their neighbors carry—without exposing people to conditions which will lay heavier and less tolerable burdens upon them. Instead . . . but the list is endless. Bonhoeffer has summed it all up when he said that God does not give us everything we want but that we can depend upon his promises.

Bonhoeffer never spoke of human creativity but only of human responsibility. In the matter of conducting ourselves as mature persons, God wants us "to come of age." This "secular Christian" did not believe that we create anything. When we trust in God's faithfulness, he creates in us praise for himself.

13. No Friend of the World: The Church and "Social Salvation"

But woe, woe to the Christian Church if it would triumph in this world, then it is not the Church that triumphs but the world has triumphed. Then the heterogeneity of Christianity and the World is done away with, the World has won, Christianity lost. Then Christ is no more the God-man, but only a distinguished man whose life is homogenous with the development of the race. Then eternity is done away with, and the stage for the perfection of all is transferred to the temporal.

Søren Kierkegaard

Bonhoeffer spoke of fearful, weak Christians, concerned only to get to heaven after death and leaving this wicked world to its own devices. Today, anyone speaking about personal salvation and believing that the primary mission of the church is saving souls is dismissed as not simply weak but rather avoiding the real world. Personal salvation, so the current view in many churches has it, cannot be separated from social salvation. Social salvation, indeed, is the biblical message, and individual salvation the invention of old-fashioned pietism. Apparently, not to be in the front ranks of those cheering the churches on to engage in bringing social justice to our world is undoubtedly a betrayal of Christ. He said, "As you did it to

115

one of the least of these my brethren, you did it to me" (Matt. 25:40 RSV).

Clearly then, in some contemporary churches Christianity is all about feeding the hungry, clothing the naked, and helping the poor and the outcasts of society, the disadvantaged and the oppressed. Since people are poor, hungry, ill-clothed, and downtrodden mainly because of the large-scale organization of society—because of social structures—then it follows that today's Christian must be concerned first of all with social sins. The fact that Christ spoke only of *one* of his brethren meant, of course, that *one* effort to relieve the oppressed showed the right spirit. Multiply the help, and that would be far more meritorious. If Christ himself did nothing visible about changing the social structures of his age, that was because such action was hardly possible in those days. In our own day, working for such change is not only possible but imperative.

That Christianity *is* about relieving suffering and the effects of poverty is something the Christian church has recognized from the first. The work done in the modern world by hospitals, asylums, and the social services generally is the continuation—on a much grander scale—of the work done previously by the churches. When the churches lost their position as the chief refuge of people in need, and the state and many voluntary agencies took over, large holes were left in the net of social protection provided by these guardians of public welfare. The churches no longer had their former preeminence in service, but they remained needed as servant churches.

It might have been thought that the churches would see themselves in the modern world continuing their traditional task: preaching the gospel, building up local Christian communities, and loving the neighbor in concrete service gladly given where the greatest need lay. During the last century, the Salvation Army was founded to take up this task in the great urban centers among people who had been passed by in the rush to reap the spoils of progress. It has never departed from its original purpose, and on that account has kept the respect and admiration of the unbelieving world. But the churches seemed to want something else. One of the marks of the new stage in creation which we have reached, according to M. M. Thomas, is participation in power structures by hitherto submerged groups. Perhaps the leaders of the churches felt that the Christian church had now become one of these groups. Things had changed vastly since the Middle Ages, when the Western Church stood at the center of power and popes were not only the spiritual rulers of Christendom but also powerful princes in their own right. The one avenue to power now seemed participation in the political process.

The social gospel provided an interpretation of the gospel that permitted the churches to say that feeding the hungry and binding up the wounded meant initiating social change. Democratic institutions provided the converted with forums for preaching the social gospel, so that their sermons could be heard not simply locally but also nationally—even internationally. Liberal Christians up to the brink of World War II earnestly argued that war might yet be averted if the nations listened to the churches and took the way of Jesus to heart, substituting love for national rivalries.

Up to the end of the nineteenth century, Protestant churches seldom if ever made official pronouncements on national policies or international issues. They left that to individual members, many of whom, of course, were identified with particular causes and frequently held some public office. As the social gospel spread, all that changed. Denominational assemblies passed resolutions and made recommendations to governments, while church leaders made pronouncements on subjects ranging from economic reform to breast-feeding— making it clear that they were speaking in their official capacities, presenting the *Christian* viewpoint. This dubious tradition has continued ever since. Only the rise of the radical theologies of the sixties increased expectations among the church leaders of what political involvement could achieve. The coming of liberation theology and its allies in the seventies resulted in salvation being defined most often in wholly political terms.

The phrase current among the churches for years is that the Christian church should be a "servant church." The phrase probably became popular through the writings of Bonhoeffer, with special reference to what he called his "nonreligious interpretation" of Jesus as "the man for others." In itself, nothing could be more appropriate for the church than to follow the Lord who came as a servant and to be known as existing to serve. The title of the pope, after all, is Servant of the Servants of God. The rub comes when the phrase is thought to mean primarily *agent of social change*—that the church is to serve the world and what the world most needs is radical change.

But are the churches commissioned by Christ to serve the world, as Bonhoeffer seems to be saying they are? Confusions may easily arise here, because the word "world" has more than one meaning.

In the Old Testament the world is simply the earth and its inhabitants. Not so in the New Testament. The New Testament introduces a new concept: this world. Sometimes *this world* is the world in the sense of a structured whole *(kosmos)*. Sometimes *this world* is literally *this age (aion)*. Whichever Greek word is used, the meaning is the same: an organized entity opposed to the rule of God. The disciples of Jesus would be perfectly familiar with the concept of this age, knowing it to be the name for the time from the Fall until God brings in his heavenly kingdom. Christian Gnostics would have interpreted this age as the age still under the rule of the demiurge and his aeons (so-called because they were eternal spirits). Most often in the New Testament, however, the world is not specifically called *this world*. Then it refers perhaps to the inhabited world, perhaps to the world organized in opposition to God.

In some New Testament passages there is an intended play on words, making *the world* hover between the two quite different meanings. The best known of these occurs in the prologue to St. John's Gospel: "He was in the world, and the world was made through him, yet the world knew him not" (Jn. 1:10 RSV). *The world* which did not recognize the Word made flesh was— and was not—the world made through the Word. The people

118

who rejected their Redeemer were created beings living in the created world. They were "in the world." At the same time they were "of the world"—a very different thing. They had given their allegiance to *this world* and thus had made themselves enemies to God and his Christ. In the letters of the New Testament *the world* almost always means *this world*. "Do not love the world or the things in the world. If any one loves the world, love for the Father is not in him" (1 Jn. 2:15 RSV). "But far be it from me to glory except in the cross of our Lord Jesus Christ, by which the world has been crucified to me, and I to the world" (Gal. 6:14 RSV).

Christian Gnostics would have agreed that no awakened spirit could possibly love the world, so that any warning on that score was really quite unnecessary. Being crucified to the world was also an excellent statement of their beliefs. The reference, of course, could not be to an actual cross of wood upon which Jesus suffered (no pure spirit could suffer), but to the boundary marking off the demiurge's terrain from that now won back for the supreme God. But the statement that "God so loved the world" (Jn. 3:16) would have been quite incomprehensible. God could only love his own, the spiritual sparks temporarily separated from the kingdom of light. Today, modern Christian Gnostics seem to be able to love the world and wish to serve it. Yet the difference between them and their second century counterparts is not so great as might at first appear.

The term *social salvation*, to begin with, points to a belief that the world needs saving. It is not lovable as it is but sinful; or, if speaking about sin is too traditional for man today, we could say it is a world full of oppressive establishments, a world that so far has failed to bring humanization. Whoever is a friend to the world as it is cannot be a person filled with Christian love. On the other hand, a person who is not active in the world, engaged in changing it, is other-worldly (if a Christian) or clinging to the past (whether a Christian or not).

The great difference between the old and new Christian Gnostic is that the latter has discarded the concept of the world as a *cosmos*, a structured whole. While the Graeco-Roman world

119

generally regarded the cosmos as the source of all good, a living being with a soul and in its every part exhibiting the pattern of good order, the old Gnostics saw it as wholly evil and oppressive. Salvation was escape from the world. The new Gnostics, thinking in temporal instead of spacial terms, see salvation as escape from the past. So the evil order from which they seek to escape is no longer called the world. The world, they say, is good. It is simply the present state of the world that is evil.

Because the new Gnostic approach to the world is essentially process, this leads to a great deal of confusion when Christian Gnostics try to interpret the Bible. For the scriptural approach to the world is both spacial and temporal. On the one hand, it is the place where we live, God's creation. This place, however, has been spoiled by human sin. *The world* is now the place which human sin has turned into *this world*—a place where the people inhabiting it do not obey the will of God. On the other hand, the world is not static but moving from the past to the future. Viewed in terms of time, *this world* is *this age,* an era already passing away and to be followed by the age of God's kingdom, an age already "at hand" (Mk. 1:15). Confusion arises when modern Christian Gnostics speak either about the world or about the kingdom, because they virtually ignore the spacial aspect which the Bible takes account of and concentrate upon the temporal aspect alone.

Of course, in their ordinary speech Christian Gnostics speak about the world extended in space. They could hardly live in the world and not do that. They will say, for example, that movements of liberation began in the Third World, but are now becoming worldwide. Yet when it comes to salvation, they think wholly in temporal terms. Salvation means the coming of the kingdom and the kingdom lies in the future.

Supporters of the social gospel began this concentration upon the future, or at least they gave it widespread currency among the churches. Its beginnings lay in the Enlightenment and acceptance of the dogma of inevitable progress. (Enlightenment thinkers introduced the concpet of the world as process when they said that we are not enlightened but we are *becoming* enlightened.) With the arrival of liberation theology, belief in the kingdom as the future of the process to be realized in world history became explicit. Salvation was now defined as effecting an exodus from the past and its oppressive establishments.

Another confusion arises at this point. In the Bible, the kingdom is coming, but it is not coming in the development of the world process. It is not the future as such. The coming of the kingdom is discontinuous with this age. When God brings in his kingdom, it is a new heaven and a new earth (Rev. 21:1). The kingdom is both a new time and a new place. The powers of the future are not headed for the kingdom (as Jürgen Moltmann, for instance, imagines) after they have won victory over the powers of the past. They are headed for *judgment*. After the Last Judgment, God's kingdom will be given. The Christian hope is not in the future at all. It is hope in the righteousness of God which never varies and will finally be revealed in glory.

Here it is instructive to note that when St. Paul speaks of the powers that try in vain to separate us from the love of God in Christ Jesus our Lord (Rom. 8:37-39), he does not mention the past at all. He mentions "things present" and "things to come." So the future is one of the evil powers of this world. It does not liberate. All our efforts to arrive at *the future God* are therefore futile. The notion of social salvation through either a gradual improvement of the conditions of human life (the social gospel) or through revolutionary change (liberationism) is completely contrary to all scriptural teaching. It is a surrender to the spirit of this age. It is friendship with the world and enmity with God. It is hatred for God's creation.

Bonhoeffer remarked that everyone seemed able to talk about the ideal society, or in religious terms, the kingdom of God, as though they knew exactly what it must be like. Yet nobody, when questioned, could agree about what it would mean in specific terms. When today believers in the world as a machine for progress speak about humanization or socialization or personalization, they are saying precisely nothing. These abstractions will feed no one, clothe no one, and certainly will comfort no one when the time of death arrives. The belief that we should sacrifice the present for the future which we only hope will come some day is not only foolish. It is also immoral.

The immorality of the belief that the kingdom will arrive in the future of this world is hardly surprising when we consider its origins. The ancient world believed (apart from the Jews and the Christians) that the cosmos provided the model for all virtues. Its order, constancy, and beauty—its soul—should be copied in the lives of humans. They too ought to live lives of orderliness, dependability, and beauty. The love of truth sprang from the desire to understand the principles underlying the cosmos, and from the search after truth would come the supreme virtue of wisdom. The old Gnostics hated the cosmos, and so for them all the classical virtues, none of which they sought, were merely the fruits of serving the demiurge. Breaking free from the oppression of the world meant breaking all established rules of conduct. The sole virtue was scorning the cosmos and its orderliness.

Jews and Christians drew their patterns of behavior from the will of God, not from the cosmos. It was God who was constant and sure, the sole source of truth and of the beauty of holiness. To obey him was wisdom. So Jews and Christians sought to be righteous rather than virtuous, although they recognized that the virtuous pagan might be not far from the kingdom. St. Paul rejected the very idea that when we accepted the free grace that came through the cross of Christ we no longer tried to follow God's righteous commands. "Are we to sin because we are not under law but under grace? By no means! . . . having been set free from sin, [you] have become slaves of righteousness" (Rom. 6:15,18 RSV). Here Christians stood firmly in the Jewish tradition. Christian Gnostics, though, rejected that tradition. Breaking the laws of righteousness means liberation from the cosmic order.

Modern Christian Gnostics do not curse the Ten Commandments. They merely point out that these were thought good in the past but are not for man today. If we are to speak about sin at all, we must draw up our own list of sins against the contemporary consciousness. The foremost among these sins is anything at all we feel to be oppressing us. Thus, by a different route the new Gnostics reach the same conclusions as the old.

Christians of the social gospel days were highly moral people, not to say moralistic. That was because the world around them was full of people living by the ethical code surviving from Victorian times. Contemporary Christian Gnostics have lived through the repudiation of Victorian prudery, experienced the so-called sexual revolution, and have come to view all morality as class morality, and therefore suspect if not totally corrupt. Being ethical has come to mean having the approved political outlook. If Christians live by love (their understanding of what is loving conduct), then no rules for living are required. Christians, says Harvey Cox, live by the gospel and not the law. The gospel is what liberates; the law is everything binding us to the past.

The necessary conclusion to be drawn from the Christian Gnostics' accumulative total of beliefs is plain. It is that the churches are to serve this age and, in this way, find mastery over this world. The churches are to participate with the world in bringing about social salvation, contributing their spiritual energy to the task. They are not to obey the God who gave his commands in the past but to work for the arrival of the future God. And their hope is not in the age to come when God gives his kingdom but in an earthly utopia which will be the culmination of this age, the age into which we are being born.

Kierkegaard, who was scarcely one of Bonhoeffer's fearful, weak Christians, saw in his time the churches turning to love the world and hoping to triumph in the world. He concluded, knowing what the Scriptures had said about friendship with the world being enmity with God, that this course could only lead to the loss of the gospel. He concluded " . . . the perfection of all is transferred to the temporal." For he had noted how modern Gnostics deified the world process and therefore subordinated everything else to time.

If Christians are to recover faith in the gospel, they must understand very clearly how being friends of the earth and being friends of the world are antithetical. The church of Jesus

123

Christ is no friend of the world, although it lives in the world. And if the churches accept the abstract agenda of the Gnostic type proposed for them, they are no friends of the earth.

In my next chapter I shall be looking at the *content* of the theory of social salvation, which will require speaking about the traditional approach to society. This approach is not abstract, for it begins with actual women and men and how they meet in social relationships. It is worldly in that it deals with sinful people in a sinful world, but it does not view people from the perspective of this world or of this age. It looks at what they are and what they could be in relationship to the will of God and in light of the kingdom which is not of this age.

14. An Ordered Neighbor-Love

We who are strong ought to bear with the failings of the weak, and not to please ourselves; let each of us please his neighbor for his good, to edify him. For Christ did not please himself.

Romans 15:1-3 RSV

The Christian life is an ordered life. . . . Service of God means that our life receives an orientation. Faith means that the one thing is enjoined us and another forbidden us. . . . The ordinance which governs the Christian life cannot be our private concern.

Karl Barth

In any process, nothing matters except the finished product. The raw materials are of no account. If you say, "I like these eggs too much to break them," you cannot make an omelet—the process will never get started. A general engaging in a battle hopes to win it, no matter how many of his troops become casualties in the process. If he loses the battle, he still hopes to win the war by expending the rest of his troops.

Process thinkers never mention this basic fact about all processes. If indeed we are entering a new stage in the creation process, as today we are being assured on many sides, we can be sure of one thing: God, or fate, or the Material World Process, or whatever is responsible for the nature of the process is concerned with nothing else except advancing to the next stage. The instructions read, stage three: throw into the heated pan a cupful of finely chopped onions; or throw in six more companies of infantry; or throw in a couple of hundred generations of human beings. The instructions do not have to state the obvious, namely, that if the end product proves to be unsatisfactory, there are always garbage heaps or mass graves available to receive the waste material.

Teilhard de Chardin's guard must have been down when he let slip the news that his universe evolving towards spirit, the machine for progress, was processing *units*. Yet any theory concerning human life that starts by assuming pure spirit to be the nature of ultimate reality is compelled to regard individual human beings as nothing more than raw material to be processed and therefore at all times fully expendable. Christian faith does not start from the belief that there is an abstract ultimate reality. It starts from the revelation given in the Hebrew scriptures, "In the beginning, God. . . ." This God is personal, a trinity of persons, and the Creator of individual human beings. Each and every individual is uniquely valuable, because to disregard the smallest part of God's good creation is to disregard to Creator. And this particular part, the individual, has been made in God's image. Even though the image has been defaced by sin, it can never be annulled; God is constant, though we are not. He fulfils his promises.

As Christians believe in a personal God, so they also try to keep their speaking about God personal. There is much talk in the churches today about learning to "think theologically." Yet theologians of the Christian church traditionally have regarded theology as nothing more than a supplement to prayer and preaching—and, in a sense, a necessary evil in a sinful world. Theological language is always to some extent abstract language, and therefore to a degree it distorts the concrete message of the gospel unless it returns continually to the words of Scripture.

Looking at the rejection of Gnostic teaching by the second-century church, F. C. Burkitt argues that it was a rejection of a theological system—very believable at the time, very up-to-date—in favor of an unsystematic tradition. That tradition, having its focus in the Scriptures, was annalistic, a record of things done and said in the past and of former people, places, and happenings. Even when regarded as the history of God's self-revelation, first to Israel, and then to the church of Jesus Christ, the Scriptures looked untidy. Some of the material preserved seemed to have no direct bearing on this history: for example, Ecclesiastes and the Song of Solomon. Yet tradition was respected and put above any later wish for relevance. The church existed to pass on a record of an historic faith, not a theology.

In other words, the church did not please itself. It tried to remain faithful to what it had received. And the sense of being under orders is something belonging to the very lifeblood of the Christian church. The thinking or theology of individual Christians goes astray whenever this sense is absent in them, even when they are not thinking about religious matters but about worldly things: human society, for instance.

Karl Barth has argued that God's creation of heaven and earth was not ended until Adam spoke the first words of his recorded in Genesis. These words concerned Eve, whom Adam called "bone of my bones and flesh of my flesh" (Gen. 2:23). Here it was recorded that God did not create human beings to be lonely individuals but to live in relationship and to confess that, without an intimate relationship to another person, no one was complete. In the case of an individual man and an individual woman, this relationship included a bodily relationship, a unity in sexual love that enriched both while it left the individuality of the two intact. Human beings as such were meant to enter into relationships, into community. For a community was formed once a couple had children and lived beside other couples.

In the Christian view, a community essentially is made up of individuals. A community is not an organism and it is not a mere collection of human units. The first annuls the concrete existence of the individual person. The second annuls the subordination of individual wills to the common good that is the essence of community. A community knows nothing of abstract

127

equality. Each member of a community is unique, and each does not please herself or himself. A community is a harmony of ordered lives, one where each individual seeks the good of the others.

Christians see the earthly community as the reflection of the heavenly community. God the Father, Son, and Holy Spirit live in a harmony of unity inconceivable to us and thus not to be reduced to the pattern of the earthly family made up of father, mother, and children. As in Christ there is neither male or female but only children of God, so the persons of the Trinity are neither male nor female. The biblical tradition calls all three persons "he" and reserves "she" for the church, the bride of Christ. It is a matter of convenience only, but one having the advantage of making us remember that there is never a one-to-one parallel between ourselves on earth and the heavenly kingdom.

Yet were no parallels possible, God would be a Gnostic unknown God and not the God who graciously reveals himself. One parallel we may safely make is that of *subordination*. In the heavenly community, the Son subordinates himself to the Father and the Spirit puts himself at the service of both the Father and the Son. (The mystery of the life within the Trinity has defeated the thinking of Christian theologians, as far as the Spirit's dependency is concerned. Eastern and Western branches of the church have been divided for centuries on this issue.) Christ, when he took on human flesh, did so because eternally he never demanded equality with the Father (Phil. 2:16). And those Christians who have wished to show that Christ never claimed to be God have always quoted the words of Jesus, "The Father is greater than I" (Jn. 14:28); yet these words actually assume the divinity of the Son.

Where abstract, mathematically imagined equality is claimed for individuals, community is made impossible. In communities, the strong protect the weak, the wise teach the less wise, and the unique character of each individual is recognized. For the weak have strengths the strong do not possess; those thought foolish can often instruct the wise, and so on. Nevertheless, within any given community there must always be those who (generally) give orders and those who (generally) obey willingly. As Barth says, the Christian life is an ordered life, and there can be no order except when some things are permitted and other things forbidden. Thus there have to be leaders who serve the community from positions of authority. Such individuals give commands, saying *yes* and *no*. Those on the receiving side of the commands may think themselves oppressed. Because sin is omnipresent they may be right. On the other hand, they may be simply voicing their own sinful unwillingness to take orders from anyone at all.

A community of persons can hardly exist except when the community is small enough to allow all the members to know one another by name. In a small community problems of organization can be discussed, and clashes between different viewpoints or different personalities can be resolved. As one member rejoices, all rejoice; as one mourns, all mourn. Common love and common loyalties unite the community. Churchgoers are frequently aware of the difficulty of keeping a community spirit once a congregation reaches a certain size and begins to seem impersonal.

There are also, however, communities which may be called great communities. In such communities, no one can possibly know all the members, for the greater number are no longer among the living. Such communities are held by a common memory uniting its members—very frequently a memory of the time when the community was small. The memory possessed by great communities is so strong that it overrides all present differences of outlook or social position among their members. A nation is one great community. A community of faith is another.

Nations are commonly hardly communities at all, but rather collections of people living together in certain territories. Often they are made up of people of varied ethnic descent, having diverse traditions and different religious and political beliefs. A nation usually becomes aware of being a community only when its existence is threatened. In wartime the spirit of a nation is made visible. During World War II, the USSR resisted invasion by Germany and survived not by rallying around Marxist ideology but by loyalty to the memory of Mother Russia. The spirit of a nation is not an abstract idea, because it is rooted in common memories having living force in the present. Loyalty to the national spirit is also loyalty to one's neighbors and companions and to those in authority in the nation. A community of faith is similarly united by these kinds of loyalties.

Christians choose to belong to different Christian denominational bodies. Yet they all claim to belong to the church of Jesus Christ. The common memory of the churches is Jesus and his small band of disciples, a little community united in calling Jesus Master and Lord. Jesus founded his church, and churches multiplied and became disunited. Unity among the churches, when it was achieved at all, was a unity imposed from above by state organization. Ecclesiastical control depended, in the last resort, upon state power. When Europe became a collection of national states, then national churches sprang into existence. The Roman church kept alive loyalty to the community of Christendom, a loyalty overriding national boundaries; the traditions of the Catholic way of life remained strong in spite of the fact that, within the different countries of Europe (and afterwards in America, north and south), national types of Catholicism became very evident. The Protestant churches, largely because they wished to return to the New Testament pattern of the small, personalized community, divided into hundreds of denominational bodies.

When people say that they want nothing to do with *organized religion,* they are wanting an abstract, ideal community of faith that could never exist on this earth. Great communities as well as small ones always have concrete existence. The church of Jesus Christ remains on earth—and Christians believe it will always remain there, for Jesus Christ promised that "the gates of hell" (i.e., death) would not prevail against it (Matt. 16:18). But it remains in the form of organized denominations. A single Christian can worship God, for indeed we always worship out of the resources provided by our individual faith. But the effective love of the neighbor requires an organized community. The gospel can be proclaimed and Christian love built up only in the churches.

John Wesley used to say that the New Testament knows nothing of a solitary Christian. In the churches where he preached the forgiveness of sins through the cross of Christ, he also organized local communities of service to the poor, the hungry, and the ill-clothed. Love of God and love of neighbor go together. Wesley also spoke out boldly against oppressive social institutions as an early opponent of the slave trade, which in those days has one reason for Britain's growing prosperity. Yet he never imagined for one moment the mission of Christ's church to be changing social conditions. In politics, as a matter of fact, he was a Tory or conservative and disliked the Whigs or liberals who were the reform party of the time. For him, neighbor love was always to be expressed concretely in terms of helping individuals. Political action could only frame large policies which might or might not liberate people from the concrete evils by which they were actually oppressed.

Jesus told his parable of the Good Samaritan in answer to the question, "And who is my neighbor?" The parable spoke of our neighbor being anyone whom we meet in our journey through life, not just someone belonging to our communities of family, neighborhood, race, or religion. It gave no warrant for any social gospel, since it spoke soley of an individual personally encountered. The parable assumed the existence of communities, however, since without these there would have been no inn to which the Samaritan could take the wounded traveler. The innkeeper would not have trusted the Samaritan to pay the balance of the traveler's bill unless he thought of him as *his* neighbor and therefore likely to honor his promise and return with the payment. Every community builds trust on a personal basis.

Barth says that the ordinance governing the Christian life cannot be our private concern. By this he means that the Christian life is lived in the Christian community. As Christians, we belong first of all to the small community of our local church, and, through that community, to the great community of the church of Jesus Christ. We do not make our own rules for living the Christian life. Our private ideas about what is good and what

131

is evil are very limited and reflect our personal prejudices. There are times when our conscience says *no* to what other Christians are doing. But the wise course is almost always the course of obedience to the decisions of the Christian community. We are not to please ourselves. Our Christian duty is to respect the authority of the community so long as the community does not flagrantly depart from the Christian tradition and from obedience to the will of God revealed in Jesus Christ.

Christians belong to other communities as well as to the community of the church. They belong to the national community, the local communities, urban or rural, and to communities of special concern. A local sports club or bird-watchers' association usually is a genuine community, a focus of loyalty and a place where individuals learn to live as good neighbors to one another. A community does not need to have lofty aims or spiritual purposes. On God's earth anything that binds us to the earth and our earthly existence is good, because it binds us to our neighbors and helps us to become better neighbors.

Yet most of the social organizations we belong to are not communities in the genuine sense of the term; that is, groups of people coming together to engage in the kind of living that edifies or builds up a common life. They are organizations brought into being for the purpose of helping their members to get what they want. Political parties are the most obvious of organizations, and professional or business or workers' organizations are all political parties in essence. They should be called collectivities rather than communities, since their purpose is to advance the self-interest of their members. Those who joins collectivities are united simply because their private ambitions for themselves agree with the private ambitions of others. They are concerned with the common good only to the extent that a greedy power group is more effective than a greedy individual can be standing alone. An expression of the collectivist creed was given some years ago by the individual who said, "What is good for General Motors is good for the country." Substitute for General Motors any other group interest—the business community, the working classes, womens' rights, rate-payers associations, the churches—and what you have is always some collectivity.

Collectivities are not evil—far from it. In a sinful world they are completely necessary. Without them, all that is stagnant and repressive in our traditional modes of life would remain unreformed and evils would multiply unchecked. The declared aim of all collectivities (other than anti-social ones) is social justice. Social justice is an ideal that can never be realized on this earth, for it is an abstract ideal. That is no reason for not striving to realize it so far as is practicable. Yet at the same time, it is completely necessary to remember that no collectivity is ever concerned with the common good lived in community. First and foremost, it wants its own agenda accepted. It wants to please itself.

Wherever people actually come together, some sort of community is born. It can never be otherwise in God's good creation. No one can meet someone else and not to some degree recognize that person as a neighbor. Hence the old saying, "There is honor among thieves." The drug community continues to exist because it generates a sense of loyalty called out by its need to avoid being wiped out by the police, the community of law and order. It is not concerned with social justice, of course, but it thinks its oppression to be utterly unjustified and fights for its right to exist. For many, political loyalty is the supreme loyalty and constitutes the principal reason for living. While very few can actually equate that abstraction "the party" with God or be willing to die for it, for many their political ideals are closely bound up with the actual community of homeland. For this community brave souls have always been ready to die without question. Patriotism is one of the oldest forms of religion.

Christians can love their country and be prepared to die for it without turning their patriotism into a religion. Much less are they prepared to turn a political party into a god to be worshipped. Yet, since political involvement is often judged today to be the principal duty of every Christian and the chief mission of the church, the function of politics in the Christian perspective becomes an important subject to consider carefully and clearly. This subject will occupy us in the next chapter.

15. The Peace of Babylon the Great

If you leave aside righteousness, what are kingdoms but great bands of brigands?

St. Augustine of Hippo (354-430)

All systems, rules and laws governing social relations are on the one hand instruments of mutuality and community; and they contain on the other hand mere approximations to, and positive contradictions of, the ideal of brotherhood.

Reinhold Niebuhr

Social gospel Christians invented social salvation. Their justification of it was this: God is loving; society today is selfish; Christians must set an example which will transform society and build the kingdom of love on earth. In our own day, "salvation" and "kingdom" are widely considered words meaningless in a secular world. So a revised justification is given for Christians taking social action to be their primary task. It goes like this: God is just; society today is unjust; Christians must work to create a just society; true Christian action is political action.

In the beginning was the deed. On that the earlier and the later Christian social activists are agreed. According to the Bible, the first human deed initiating social change was when Cain killed his brother Abel. Cain, condemned by God to be a wanderer over the earth, went on to found the first city (Gen. 4:17).

What we today call politics is the activity belonging to life in the city *(polis)*. The city is the place where collective life begins. While early cities were settlements where people of a common stock having common traditions gathered, from the first they were also places where wanderers found a refuge. There conquered peoples brought back as slaves could after a time become citizens; so races and traditions mingled. Thus the city is the creation of the human will. The will which is also deed says, "Let there be the city." Since human beings cannot create anything original—anything not already on the earth God has made—so the city is inevitably the reflection of sinful human nature. The city is the embodiment of the selfish will to have its own kingdom instead of God's kingdom. So the kingdoms of this world arise, built like the tower of Babel in the effort to reach up to heaven. In Jewish legend, archers standing on the top of that tower shot arrows up to heaven, and drops of blood representing the sorrow of the Lord fell down upon them.

The city and its politics exist on earth; therefore they are not evil. The good of the city is the impulse towards true community found in a life that mostly achieves only collectivity. That is why St. Augustine, the great Christian father of the Latin Western Church, spoke of righteousness being present in the kingdoms of this world. In Augustine's lifetime, the city of Rome had fallen before the advancing armies of the barbarian tribes from the territories east and north of the borders of the Roman empire. Soon they were to engulf the whole empire. As St. Augustine lay dying, his own city of Hippo in North Africa was under siege. After Rome fell, citizens of the empire (officially Christian for almost a century) blamed the new religion. The city had flourished under the old gods, and now the god of the Christians had been unable to save it. St. Augustine sought to reply to these accusations in *The City of God* (312-426), one of the great books of all time and the first Christian treatise on political philosophy.

135

St. Augustine drew upon biblical symbolism. In the Old Testament, Babylon became after the Exile the name given to all the gentile powers that had oppressed Israel. Jerusalem, the city of David, stood for the hope of Israel in the God who had promised his people permanent peace and freedom. In the New Testament, the new Jerusalem would arrive after Babylon had been dethroned: "Fallen, fallen is Babylon the great!" (Rev. 18:2 RSV). St. Augustine spoke of the two cities—intermingled on earth yet eternally distinct. Jerusalem was the city raised by the love of God to the neglect of self. Babylon was the city raised by the love of self in defiance of God.

Although wicked, Babylon's rulers were "the powers that be" and "ordained of God" (Rom. 13:1 KJB; JB—"government comes from God"). God had intended the human race to live in community. Then sin came into the world, and humans pleased themselves. They achieved only collectivity. Yet God still was Lord of the earth. So at the heart of collectivity lay a kernel of community, the community people still longed for in spite of themselves. Jerusalem was present even in Babylon. God had ordained that his children would be ruled by force since they would not be ruled by his gracious will. If they refused an ordered neighbor love, then they must endure being organized by state power. For the power of rulers prevented the total lack of order which would follow if individuals were free to please themselves without restraints. In God's creation, there are always limits set for the good of all. The kingdoms of this world behaved as antisocial persons (brigands) behaved, except that the kernel of righteousness remained within them and therefore civilized societies could be nurtured by them.

St. Augustine's name for community (my own term) was the biblical word "people." In the Old Testament, when Israel disobeyed the Lord, he refused to call them *his people*. St. Augustine said that a people can hardly exist unless the one true God is worshipped. Thus he was reluctant to call the citizens of old pagan Rome *a people*. Yet he realized that, since all members of the human race are aware of a distinction between good and evil and feel some obligation to obey the voice of conscience,

136

human beings can obey God even when they do not believe in him. Every organized group or nation, therefore, is in some sense of the word *a people*. But there is no real hope for this world until belief in the Creator and Redeemer is consciously acknowledged among all nations. The institutions set up by worldly powers are necessarily oppressive. They can liberate individuals and the whole body of citizens to a certain extent, insofar as they encourage righteousness. But the Christian church alone represents the Jerusalem that is from above. Obedience to the church is the way of permanent liberation, the guarantee of true peace and ordered neighbor love.

Both Catholics and Protestants look back to *The City of God* and claim it as their own. Catholics see in it support for their claim that the state must protect and support the church and abide by its moral teachings; otherwise the state is unrighteous and must be opposed. Protestants read St. Augustine's book rather differently. For them, the Church organized on earth in various churches does not speak with the full authority of Christ himself. The churches, being influenced by the spirit of the world, are imperfect. They may ask the state to listen to them on matters of the public good but cannot order it to do so. After all, St. Augustine admitted that Babylon and Jerusalem are never perfectly separated in this world; and, speaking of the church, he said, "There are many sheep outside the fold, and many wolves within."

One modern Protestant much indebted to St. Augustine was Reinhold Niebuhr, professor of Applied Christianity at Union Seminary, New York, from the late 1920s into the 1960s. Niebuhr was brought up within the atmosphere of the American social gospel, and he remained grateful for the movement's emphasis upon bringing Christian faith to bear upon the world's problems, even though he spent much of his time fighting liberal Christianity. Against the liberals, he argued that no amount of goodwill would ever change an unloving society into a loving one. The state and its social institutions are by nature self-regarding. Nations have but one end: to keep themselves in being. Governments, if they are wise, will further the rule of justice to undergird their power; yet their inclination is always to put power before justice. Individuals alone, using the opportunities afforded them, can guide institutions to seek the good of all. In *Moral Man and Immoral Society; A Study in Ethics and Politics* (1932), Niebuhr set out this thesis fully. He never departed from it.

Niebuhr read Kierkegaard, and, with some reservations, he admired Karl Barth. He was considered by Bonhoeffer a philosopher of religion. In addition, he was a child of the Ritchlian tradition seeing Christianity as "the religion of Jesus." For him, "the Jesus of history is a perfect symbol of the absolute in history." Yet he gave us as clear an exposition of how Jerusalem differs from Babylon as anyone in our century has supplied. The idea of evil being human energy on its way to perfecting the future was not for him. He saw the universe as a place where good and evil stand forever in opposition, however much we ourselves may confuse the two and mistake our good intentions for the insight of "pure spirit." Social and political thinkers and professional politicians of his generation confessed themselves indebted to him for clarifying the issues they had to deal with in their own fields of discipline.

Niebuhr's language, though, was sometimes puzzling. In his most comprehensive work, the two volume *The Nature and Destiny of Man* (1941, 1943), he spoke of inordinate self-love being *unnatural*, a false relationship to both the temporal and eternal. He might have been a Greek, speaking of the failure to learn from the order of the cosmos to keep our desires within the bounds of moderation. Yet in the next sentence he went on to say, "If man knew, loved and obeyed God as the author and end of his existence, a proper limit would be set for his desires, including the natural impulse of survival." Nothing could be more Christian than this latter sentence, making us wonder why he did not speak of inordinate self-love being the temptation to make ourselves gods—the temptation to invent our own religion, one deifying the human spirit. Perhaps he may have wished to show how Christians could think biblically without being restricted to the words of the Bible. His aim was always to speak to the people of his generation broadly, and not to believers alone.

Certainly Niebuhr often employed what Bonhoeffer later was to call a nonreligious interpretation of biblical terms. Thus, instead of speaking of Babylon and Jerusalem, he referred to the realm of power and the realm of love. He advised his contemporaries, "Better to accept a frank dualism in morals than to attempt a harmony between them which threatens the effectiveness of both." Failure to draw the necessary dividing lines, he observed, blinded people not only to the true nature and mission of the Christian church but also to the nature of political realities.

Niebuhr liked to call his own outlook "Christian realism." His view of social action was that it always operated politically, that is, "by setting power against power." Politics as such is amoral. If moral individuals wish to introduce moral good into the realm of power, the best they can do is to hope to hold some evils in check. Political action is always risky because it involves a choice between two evils. And which is the lesser of two evils before us is seldom very evident at the time when the choice has to be made. Politics being the art of the possible, it has necessarily to deal with the here and now in a most concrete way. Having faith in human perfectibility is folly, since it goes against all the facts. Thinking good intentions are enough is wicked folly and the surest way to turn this earth into a hell. Power being always self-regarding, the political process is a balancing of one power structure against another, a discerning of which selfish interest will do less harm at any given time and place. In the amoral realm of politics, the actions of people of good will must be directed to prevent society from going downhill into complete immorality.

Using Satan to cast out Satan may seem a procedure hopeless from the start. But of course Babylon is not Satan. As Augustine pointed out, the kingdoms of this world may resemble bands of brigands, but they also contain a kernel of righteousness. Christians operating in the political realm seek to enlarge the areas within society where righteousness lies by checking the unimpeded advance of selfish interests. As politicians, Christians have no better qualifications than unbelievers in practical terms. They have to calculate, like everybody else, where the existing balance of power lies, what are the strengths of the various power structures at any given moment, and the point at which pressure can be employed successfully to alter the present balance for something better. Their sole asset is that they are concerned with righteousness and believe that they can discern, at least in part, what is the will of God in a particular situation.

Niebuhr had much to say that was acutely observant about the disaster following the attempts of idealistic politicians and social theorists to impose some unrealistic agenda upon society. In politics, the most harm is often done by the best individuals, those who have high standards but lack the ruthlessness required in the political arena. On the other hand, persons of dubious moral character or of restricted vision of the good frequently advance the common good of a community or of a nation, simply because they possess a shrewd insight into how selfishness operates in individuals and in social groups. "The sons of this world are wiser in their own generation than the sons of light" (Lk 16:8 RSV). Niebuhr insisted that before Christians venture into the realm of politics, they had best become acquainted with the rules of the political game and learn how to play the game and win. Nothing is more futile than the idealist who laments how much he or she could have done for the world had only the world heeded. Niebuhr pointed that out to the editor of a prominent American Christian weekly, who after the outbreak of World War II, had written an editorial in which he said that Christians had not been able to stop that war, but it was still possible for them to work harder and prevent the next war!

St. Augustine and Reinhold Niebuhr both called their generations to turn away from the abstractions of religious and political rhetoric and look at the concrete conditions of life on earth. And both told their contemporaries how we cannot truly serve this world unless we see the present in the light of the world to come—God's kingdom where his righteous will is done. Here and now, Babylon and Jerusalem are realities. We stand between the two cities each of which claims our allegiance. If we see only Babylon, we are that city's slaves. If we see only Jerusalem, we are ignoring our duty to God and to our neighbor. So long as we remain on the earth, we have to live and work in the earthly city although we know that we owe our allegiance ultimately to the heavenly city, whose citizens we are.

Until Babylon falls, as it will at the time when God so ordains, Christians live in the disorder that is Babylon, contending with the many evils this disorder brings. Yet we live also in the peace of Babylon, such as it is. The peace of Babylon is the uneasy peace achieved under the protection of the big batallions or the shield of atomic weapons. "Let him who desires peace prepare for war," wrote Vegetius in the fourth century. "Talk softly and carry a big stick," advised a Roosevelt in our own century. For any sovereign state, war is simply diplomacy carried out by other means. For Babylon, her own prosperity and self-aggrandizement is the only righteousness she recognizes. Good and evil in the earthly city are the same thing as success and failure—success in getting what you want, failure when the triumph of the will is frustrated. Politics has to reckon with both events, learning how to emerge out of the failure successfully, since "he who fights and runs away/lives to fight another day." For politics is not only the art of the possible; it is also the art of bowing to the inevitable and still contriving to survive and wait for the next chance to hit back at one's enemies.

Politics is amoral, yet politicians have to seem moral; otherwise they would not be supported by individuals who believe in there being a difference between right and wrong (i.e., Niebuhr's moral man). Yet in politics nothing is done soley for moral reasons. In the American Civil War, the North felt itself righteous in that it condemned the evil of chattel slavery. The South was quick to respond that the North had an economy which did not need slaves and was ready to oppress the part of the country that depended upon slave labor for its prosperity, so that the North might grow even richer while the South grew poorer. Also, when the British created goodwill by withdrawing gracefully from India and then proceeded to grant other parts of the empire their independence, these actions seemed generous. Yet it was plain that Great Britain, exhausted from war, could no longer afford to run colonies or to meet the rising tide of nationalism in the lands she had ruled so long. These examples could be multiplied endlessly. What they demonstrate is not that politicians are all hypocrites, for they may well be motivated by real concern for moral values. They simply point to the fact that politics is about power in the last resort. Governments and all decision-makers running collectivities are forced to act to bring about, wherever possible, the triumph of the collective will. They have been put in power to advance the self-interest of social groups, and unless they serve those interests they will soon be out of power.

The peace of Babylon the Great includes the recognition of human rights. The fact that an amoral pursuit of power is forced to recognize that individuals have rights is one of the proofs that Babylon cannot hold together without some recognition of righteousness. Certainly, those individuals forming governments or other ruling bodies oppress and kill any individuals opposing them whenever they get the chance. If they do not do so, it is because the traditions of their countries or social groups forbid violent action against private citizens. The rule of law is the great civilizing achievement of Babylon, and the tradition of the citizen's right to equality before the law was one that took centuries to establish. When an individual is guaranteed this equality by the powers that be, it is about the only situation on earth where one individual is equal to another individual. Christians see it as a reflection in this world of the heavenly Father being no respecter of persons (Acts 10:34; Rom. 2:11), but counting each of his children equally dear to him.

Individual rights are one thing, but group rights are another. And when groups are granted rights upon the law—the right to free association, or to freedom of speech (of the press, for example), and so on—then such rights are dependent upon there being no threat to the body politic in the exercise of these rights. These kinds of rights are often in conflict. The right to publish anti-Semitic literature, for example, conflicts with the right to freedom of religion and the right of ethnic minorities not to be persecuted on account of their origins. The multiplication of rights that can be legally enforced is no substitute for a tradition of living which accepts the fact that neighbors are neighbors, whatever social groups to which they may belong. In a sinful world, of course, actions threatening the unity of the state require to be forbidden by specific legislation. But the moral standards of individuals in the state are always the chief safeguards of the unity of the state, and a breakdown in these standards is indicative of the presence of ill-health in the body politic.

Christians cannot ignore politics, for although they are not citizens of Babylon, they live in an age when Babylon the great has not yet fallen. They have been enrolled, willy-nilly, as citizens of the country where they were born or where they have chosen to stay. The Christian church cannot ignore politics either, yet it should not take sides in political issues. It can condemn the oppression of individual citizens. If it ventures farther it treads on dangerous ground. The danger lies not at all in the possibility that the state may resent interference in its affairs and vent its wrath upon the church. Under persecution, the church has survived many times and, most often (though not always) grown stronger. The danger lies in the church forgetting its mission. It may wish to serve the world, flattered by the praise it receives from some quarters for its *prophetic witness*. It may try to win people to its side by saying, "Look what we are doing to advance your freedoms and your rights, to protest social evils and to reduce poverty and underdevelopment, and to make the resources of the earth available to all." Insofar as the church courts Babylon in this way it loses its soul and departs from its Lord, seeking to triumph in the world by making itself look like the world's humble servant.

Because the church of Jesus Christ cares for individuals, it will be watchful also to care for those communities nurturing personal life. The churches should cry out against anti-Semitism, for example, since this evil is much more than social evil. Anti-Semitism and all similar hatreds strike at the heart of neighbor-love. Similarly, the churches should cry out against every attempt of the state to make the family a mere social convenience, forgetting that it is the place where we learn what community means, where love and trust is born, and where the heavenly community is reflected in an earthly one. Every church that is faithful to its mandate to preach the gospel will know where it can no longer give a limited *yes* to Babylon and must return an outright *no*.

On this earth nothing is simple, although a few important things are self-evident to the simple in heart. In the matter of acting as Christians in society, there will always be many gray areas where some Christians will disagree with others over what the Christian's duty is in relation to Babylon. What is most crucial here is that action should be consistent and well-ordered. If we are to protest as Christians against some particular evil, we must protest against *all* instances of this evil, not selecting a few because they are most condemned by the world around us. If we cry out against the oppression of black people by white people, we cannot overlook or condone the oppression of black people by black people or even reverse discrimination (the belief that white people should be ashamed of being white). When we work to find political means to overthrow oppressive regimes in other countries, we should not mark out a few regimes as the important ones to attack, just because we find them being condemned by acquaintances or featured prominently in the mass media. Any casual glance at the literature distributed by the churches will show how largely they depart from the rule of impartial reading of the available evidence, how often the same targets are singled out with monotonous regularity, and how little churchpeople are urged to understand the ambiguities of the situation in a country they do not know before starting to throw stones. Politicians from the beginning have known that the best way to gain an enthusiastic following is to give their audience a tangible enemy to hate. Christians are told to turn away from evil, but not to hate evildoers—rather to pray for them. But the ways of the world are attractive to even the most faithful Christians, and hatred comes much more easily than understanding, judgmental condemnation easier than willingness to confess that we do not know enough to pass judgment on others.

It is also always a temptation for us to believe that we are being treated unjustly instead of being grateful for the measure of equity we enjoy in the social order where we live. "There is great gain in godliness with contentment" (1 Tim. 6:6 RSV). Such a statement is heresy to a generation believing social change to be the chief goal of the Christian and the sole justification for the continued existence of the churches. The energetic Christian thinks contentment to be synonymous with complacency and self-righteousness. And yet thanksgiving is one of the most important elements in Christian worship, when we remember what has been done for us by God and by our fellow travelers on the way, both present and past. Babylon detests thankfulness, for her intention is to keep her slaves without time to do anything except work for her greater glory. Even rebellious slaves are more easy to manage than contented ones, for the latter may be thinking their own thoughts. They may even come to the conclusion that they do not depend upon Babylon for the resources necessary for existence. And then where would be the glory of her kingdom? Where would be those most pleasing of sounds: the flattery poured out by those who bow down before her power, and the impotent curses of rebellious slaves and enemy captives led away to punishment and death?

We know the nature of Babylon the Great, for we are very familiar with how her servants behave. Formerly, despots mounting the throne of a kingdom killed all other claimants to the throne. Today, after elections the party faithful cheer their successful leaders. The leaders, ignoring their defeated rivals, flatter the public that has elected them and vow to serve their interests well. Modern ways are more civilized, but the procedure is the same and arouses the same emotions of triumph in the victors, the same servility before success.

Social existence, however, is more than politics, and this *more* is the subject now to be considered.

145

16. In the Land of the Philistines

For freedom Christ has set us free; stand fast therefore, and do not submit again to a yoke of slavery.

Galatians 5:1 RSV

A humble but purposeful and really happy freedom of movement will always, to some degree, be allowed us even in this age—the freedom, that is, of living in the land of the Philistines: . . . in and out of the house of the state, which, call it what you will, is the beast of the bottomless pit; in and out of the house of secular social democracy; in and out of the house of falsely heralded science and the liberal arts; and finally even in and out of the house of worship.

Karl Barth

Kierkegaard said that he was living in an age when everything was being turned into politics. He also said that he was living in the age of the crowd, an age dominated by publicity and advertising which created public opinion. And, so Kierkegaard insisted, *the crowd is untruth.*

The two phenomena were closely connected. In pre-Enlightenment days, when absolute monarchy was the rule, the great princes of Europe guarded their powers jealously and refused access to the political process to all but a few. When

146

democratic regimes arrived, politicians had to court the favor of the general public, and they were not slow to discover means of manipulating public opinion in order to gain and hold power. Kierkegaard saw in his century the rise of techniques for such manipulation, particularly through the power of the popular press. For him, the crowd was untruth because it was impersonal and faceless. We know the names of people at the trial of Jesus: Pilate and Herod, Annas and Caiaphas. But we do not know the people who made up the crowd that determined the outcome of the trial by shouting for Barabbas instead of Jesus. What makes us individuals is our willingness to take responsibility for our actions. The crowd or the public is responsible to nobody. In democracies, the secret ballot is the guarantee that individuals will not be victimized for their opinions. Yet it is a symbol, as well, of the facelessness of modern life and of the triumph of the will over rational moral judgment. Our rulers do not have to be wicked or incompetent to be turned out of office. All that is needed is for the public to be tired of them.

One reason for the increasing facelessness of contemporary society has been the growth of technology. In his seminal book *The Technological Society* (ET 1964), Jacques Ellul argued that in our century technology has become so powerful that it has passed from giving us the means to achieve what we desire to dictating the ends we are to pursue. Like politicians, technocrats possess power and wish to increase this power. Since they promise the public access to the newest and the best in ways of getting what the public wants, technocrats encourage people to believe that they need nothing else in this world. The result is the consumer society, one feeding on the products of technology. With this development comes the multiplication of bureaucrats to regulate the flow of products from manufacturer to consumer and to superintend all the complex processes kept going by public demand for the newest and the best that technology offers. Power now resides, says Ellul, less in government legislation than in "an enormous machine of bureaus."

147

Jacques Ellul is a French Protestant layman, a professor of law and widely active in politics. He is also a Christian much indebted to Karl Barth for his ideas both on Christian faith and on society. He has been scathing in his *no* to the cult of the human and to all attempts to incorporate futurism and utopianism into Christianity. He speaks of the *rabies politica* that has infected the churches, an infection causing them to be blind to the difference between living in the world and being conformed to the fashions of the world; blind equally to the fact that political liberation means for the great majority of ordinary people no more than a change of oppressors.

The technological society of which Ellul writes is new in the sense that modern technology is wedded to the explosion of scientific discoveries. Yet technology as such is as old as the attempt to organize human beings efficiently to use techniques of getting things done. Technology does not recognize the existence of people; it thinks wholly in terms of production quotas and of the manpower needed to achieve these. When slave labor gave way to machines and machine-minders, technology came into its own. Almost equally ancient in its origins is bureaucracy, itself the embodiment of techniques for organizing the work of the state. The indifference of bureaucrats to individual needs and their way of reducing everything to abstract statistics provide the subject for many jokes. Nevertheless, private citizens living in a highly bureaucratized society are well aware that these are no cause for laughter.

Nor has this century, the supposedly new stage in the creation-process, been hilarious. Bloody wars involving the slaughter of civilians, genocide, deliberate starvation of populations, forcing masses from their homeland and turning them into disregarded refugees, tyranny and torture—these crimes have stained all the pages of history. But never before have they been witnessed on so large a scale as they have since World War I. Our century's symbols are the Holocaust, Hiroshima, and the killing fields of Cambodia. The technology that has lengthened the lifespan and allowed the world population to multiply has also perfected lethal weaponry and brought into being death camps, brainwashing, and countless other techniques permitting governments to keep their citizens servile. The spread of the drug culture, so evident for some time in North America but quickly becoming a worldwide phenomenon, shows how totalitarian regimes are not the only threat to our ideal of social democratic culture. Growing numbers of people in what we (with some justification) call the free world are coming to believe that life is not worth living here on earth and are seeking to fly from it into a self-created world. Becoming "high" is, in fact, the modern substitute for Gnostic salvation.

Neither drugs nor the religion of the New Age movement can change the character of our technological culture with its accompanying bureaucracies. We live in this age, and here God asks us to serve him. Were the churches to throw off their obsession with politics they would have a gospel to preach that actually liberates the present instead of one merely promising to liberate the future. As Karl Barth reminded Christians over seventy years ago, it is not the state (the beast of the bottomless pit) that gives us our freedom. Christ does that.

Reinhold Niebuhr used to say that the attitude of Christians should be one neither of optimism or pessimism concerning the future but one of living in the present without undue seriousness or soul-destroying cynicism. He called this attitude *the nonchalance of faith*. Barth, speaking in a more biblical way, simply called it *happy freedom*. The image which Barth used when he referred to the Christian life in the world of contemporary culture was an illuminating one. For Israel, the land of the Philistines represented all that was inimical to the service of the one true God. It was the place of idol worship, and because of its geographical position its rulers had as their constant policy keeping the Hebrew tribes weak and disunited. Thus Philistia was always an active threat to Israel's existence as one people of God. Living in the land of the Philistines, then, means for Christians living in a culture hostile to fidelity to Christ.

Happy Christian freedom is possible in the land of the Philistines so long as we go in and out without serving the local idols, and without adopting the national policy. Christians in Philistia can enjoy a secular life, so long as they do not bow down before the idol of secularism, the idol set up to replace the God of Jesus Christ. Christians may enter into the political life of Philistia, so long as they are free from the disease of *rabies politica,* a virulent infection spread throughout that land. So in Philistia Christians are free to become scientists, social scientists, economists, political theorists, philosophers, writers, artists, craftsmen, executives, lawyers, laborers, or professional athletes. The range of their freedom is boundless, provided they know their limitations and respect the boundaries which God has set for all human activities. All things are ours, if we are Christ's.

Philistia is Babylon in its more amiable aspect. In Babylon the Hebrews were captives, far from home and mourning the loss of Jerusalem. The Philistines were neighbors of God's people, even though they were also enemy nationals, and probably also Semites. Samson went visiting in the nearby towns across the border. David sought refuge in Philistine territory when he had to flee from Saul. Living in the land of the Philistines, then, can be a symbol of the fact that we have no choice in the matter of which culture we happen to be born into. Equally, calling our culture Philistia can be a reminder that our culture is never to be wholly trusted. Samson lost his eyes because he was blind to the treacherous nature of a woman of the Philistines; and David once narrowly escaped being forced to march against his native land at the head of a Philistine army. Simply because Philistia is milder than Babylon, it is no less dangerous.

Just as the powers that be in Babylon are ordained of God, so the present culture exists also as God's gift to us. Christians are free to use all that is good in culture, but free also not to be used by what is evil in it. And what a rich and varied culture we possess in our Western heritage, the result of many centuries and many nations! While there is much in it of which we have need to be ashamed, there is also a multitude of reasons why we should thank God for its many-faceted glories, and for the work of gifted individuals who have contributed to make it what it is today.

Almost certainly, the greatest evil in contemporary culture is the strenuous attempt presently being made to have politics swallow up all the rest of culture. The willingness to sacrifice the good things we now enjoy for the sake of an imaginary future of perfection is the sign of a final rejection of God and his good creation. It is the false religion seeking the triumph of the human will in defiance of God's will. Even the evil of a depersonalizing technological culture is second to the evil of the politicization of everything. In fact, the second evil is an offspring of the first. Like politics, technology is *a*moral, but it need not be *im*moral. Only when the pursuit of technology becomes a religion, only when it is seen as the means whereby the triumph of the will may be achieved, are the fruits of human knowledge turned into bitter fruits.

What is good in Western culture is its legacy from the past. This legacy is available to us to further, enlarge, and (where needed) correct. Its goodness lies in its respect for the individual and all that comes from the character, genius, and the humankindness of persons. Western culture is not a process leading to humanization. It is everything that we have come to associate with the names of such individuals as Homer, Plato, Aquinas, Dante, Galileo, Shakespeare, Newton, Dostoievski, Einstein, and a host of others. It is the unknown monks laboring over illuminated manuscripts in the Middle Ages, the makers of musical instruments, the politicians who devoted their lives to serving their homelands, and the mothers who brought up their children to understand the meaning of duty. Homeowners painting their homes because they want them to look their best and not because they want to impress the family next door—they too are preserving their cultural heritage. Culture is always concretely embodied in human work.

Culture builds up communities as distinct from collectivities. In the collective realms of social life all change, for better or worse, is brought about by power plays. One interest is pitted against another, and the stronger wins. Of course, since culture exists in a sinful world, it is closely bound up with the exercise of power. The history of the Christian churches is what it is because the Emperor Constantine decided, for reasons of power, to adopt Christianity as the favored religion of his empire.

American culture would never have emerged as a distinct entity had not the settlers from Europe defeated the redcoats of George III. At the same time, culture is advanced solely as it turns away from a merely collective view of society and starts to build up communities.

One of the most distinctive marks of a culture is that it plays games. Play is the taming of the desire for power. It civilizes the will to destroy the enemy, while continuing to satisfy the desire for victory. Chess, for example, is a game of mimic warfare. The piece we now call the Queen was originally called the General, and the pawns the foot soldiers. Team sports allow actual combat to take place. *We* contend against *them*, only now upon a field that is no longer a battlefield. Barbarians find only sports involving actual death sufficiently exciting. Nevertheless, in all sports and games it is always skill or luck that motivates the action—win or lose. People play for the sake of playing.

In Babylon, life is too serious for games. Gaining and keeping power is all-important, and losing is the unforgivable sin. Few party leaders, after being defeated in an election, are given the chance to try again. In the Philistia of culture, however, the desired end is joy: the joy of knowledge for its own sake; the joy of work well done; the joy of discovery and invention; and the joy of enjoyment itself. In this sense, a human being shows forth the image of the Creator—never being an original creator, of course, yet looking upon the works of her or his hands and finding them good. God, said St. Thomas Aquinas, made the world in play. In our fallen world, work is mostly laborious and often painful. Play is tiring, but it makes us seek the joy of rest. Because the activities of culture always bring us close to the earth, they help us appreciate the goodness of God's original creation and encourage us to turn in thankfulness to him.

"I know that there is no happiness for man except in pleasure and enjoyment while he lives. And when man eats and drinks and finds happiness in his work, this is a gift of God" (Eccles. 2:24). Barth refers to Ecclesiastes explicitly in connection with living among the Philistines and not serving their idols. The seeming epicureanism of the Preacher, he adds, is not at odds with the precepts of the gospels: "This is the solid and fundamental biblical perception of life." And this perception, he continues, leads to *an attack* upon the pagan ideas about human life.

Eating and drinking and working with the awareness that these things are a gift of God is certainly not characteristic of today's outlook, even among the churches. In *The Denial of Death* (1973), Ernest Becker looks at the contemporary terror of facing death as a reality for every individual and finds it to be a denial of life. Although himself holding a naturalistic philosophy, Becker turns to Kierkegaard for his diagnosis of this modern malaise. He ends by saying that people today are drinking and drugging themselves out of awareness, or doing the same thing by going shopping. "As awareness calls for types of heroic dedication that his [modern man's] culture no longer provides for him, society contrives to help him forget," concludes Becker. What Becker calls heroic dedication, Christians call following Christ and our simple duty.

Becker draws attention to the load of guilt carried by people today, causing so many to seek relief through psychiatric care. Because everything is viewed from a political perspective, Becker might have added, eating and drinking are frequently made into a reason for additional guilt. We are constantly being reminded—especially at church—that the West gluts itself on expensive meals while in the Third World millions starve. Thus the traditional grace before eating is simply one more example of the hypocrisy of Western Christianity and of its alliance with the forces of injustice. On these grounds, the Last Supper itself would stand condemned. Jesus must have forgotten his own parable of starving Lazarus as he sat with only his disciples around him in the upper room.

Yet the memory of the Last Supper, with its acted parable of footwashing, can actually be the memory removing guilt. It can be an attack upon contemporary idols, including the idol of *politics first*. It can help Christians to read Ecclesiastes as something other

153

than a treatise hardly deserving of inclusion in the Bible. It can enable believers to cut themselves loose from what Becker calls *the nexus of unfreedom* and to discover anew "the glorious liberty of the children of God" (Rom. 8:21 RSV). For living to know the heroism of the ordinary is living as children of the Lord of the earth. The unfashionable yet effective maxim adopted by the Salvation Army is, "First we feed the soul, and then we feed the body." The urgent demand of our bodies to be fed can also be the means of our discovery that we do not live by bread alone.

Culture itself is largely a matter of remembering, of being able to add to (and sometimes correct) traditions received from the past because these traditions are loved as the sources of joy. Our contemporary world preserves some thankfulness for the existence of the ordinary illumined by memory: the family meal, the laughter of friends, the welcome home at the end of a working day, the gift given with sacrificial love, or the touch of a hand extended to the distressed or the dying. These things are valued because they belong to the traditions of the good life among the Philistines (which are, for the most part, the traditions of Christendom). If they are not thought to be serious because they are not contributing to the socialization and humanization of humanity, that is because people have become, in Kierkegaard's phrase, absentminded. If we forget the concrete needs of our neighbor, whom we have seen, we are not likely to remember God, whom we have not seen (1 Jn. 4:20).

Traditions are built up of the memories of individuals and communities over many generations. They are essential to culture, for culture is cumulative—not at all the same thing as progressive. Today, scientists have advanced human knowledge about the world immensely because they carry on a tradition begun by the first individuals who were curious about the earth and the heavens. (Einstein once said, "I am not particularly intelligent, but I am very, very curious.") The scientific method was worked out by a line of scientists in which the greatest luminary was Isaac Newton. And so it is in every realm of culture. There is a tradition that is followed, and the individuals who added to this tradition are remembered as models to be followed. No poet today forgets Homer or Virgil, Chaucer or Villon, however little that particular poet may desire to copy them.

Traditions, too, are essential for daily living in society, beginning with the tradition of our common speech. A family meal is not a once-and-for-all event. It is made meaningful because it follows the traditional pattern of other meals, some of which are vividly remembered because they were the occasions of shared family joys and sorrows. For Christians, each daily event is resonant with echoes from the Scriptures. They set out on some new venture as Abraham did from Ur of the Chaldees. They groan over a thankless task or a difficult employer as Israel in Egypt groans under the taskmasters there. They mourn the death of a beloved friend as David mourned for Jonathan. They are comforted in the valley of the shadow as was the writer of the Shepherd Psalm. They walk their evening path not alone, as did the two on the Emmaus road.

If *being human* means anything at all, it means being a person having memories and so belonging to a tradition. It means reaching out to persons who may belong to other traditions but who still take the same earthly path as we do and so have similar memories. It means finding the people in the land of the Philistines to be our neighbors, even though we do not worship the same gods. It means affirming with the old pagan dramatist Terence, "I am a man, and I count nothing human indifferent to me." There are no degrees of becoming human and no process of becoming humanized. We lose our humanity only when we forget to be thankful for being on the earth and when we forget our creaturely limitations—when we aspire to be pure spirit.

Today it is often said that Jesus shows us what it means to be human. The Son of God did not have to take on human flesh to reveal to us that we are God's creatures. The Incarnation took place to reveal to us how we ought to live our our humanity in the world as children of the world that is to come. The keynote of the Incarnation is humility (Phil. 2:1-10), and not humanity. Because the Word dwelt with us, we can find here and now "a humble but purposeful and really happy freedom."

155

Karl Barth points out how earthly are the parables of Jesus: a woman loses a coin and behaves as though she had lost everything; a speculator takes the risk of investing everything in a single pearl; a king goes to war but realizes, in the nick of time, that retreat is his only safe option; a rascal makes private deals with his employer's money. Here is not idealism but mostly ordinary human emotions, often centering around greed and self-interest. The teachings of Jesus are certainly not intended to give us a vision of the sacred in the secular. Rather, they show us how worldly life is not properly understood until it is seen in the light of the world that is to come. The kingdom is *like* this earth, with sin changed into obedience to the righteous God.

The Christian belief that happy freedom comes from obedience to God's will and not from pleasing ourselves is a belief not altogether absent in the land of the Philistines. Cultural achievements are always the fruit of a disciplined life. Scientists and artists do not look to the will of God for direction, but they do look to the laws governing the order found in this earth. The athlete and the ballet dancer discipline their bodies as St. Paul told Christians to do (1 Cor. 9:24-27), with a rigor which few church people would ever attempt. Architects know that no creative imagination counts for much if they forget physical laws and their buildings collapse. In the various realms of culture, humanity is taken for granted and what is important is what people actually do with their human talents. Nothing of worth is produced by the triumph of the will. Techniques are needed; yet technique is never allowed to be more than a means to an end—and it never under any circumstances dictates the end. Servants of culture who are more than poseurs and slaves of current fashions are without exception children of the earth.

Whenever one looks at any aspect of the Christian living in society, one returns to the theme of Christian obedience. It may be useful now to turn directly to this theme.

17. Obedient Thinking

A discovery is made—the human race triumphs; full of enthusiasm everything is set in motion in order to make the discovery more and more perfect. The human race is jubilant and adores itself. At length there comes a pause—people come to a halt; but is that discovery a good, particularly in its extra-ordinary perfection! And so once again the most eminent minds are obliged to think themselves almost silly in order to discover safety-valves, dampers, drags etc., so as, if possible to stop again, so that that unparalleled and imcomparable perfect discovery, the pride of the human race, should not end by running away and desolating the whole world.

Søren Kierkegaard

We demolish arguments and every pretension that sets itself up against the knowledge of God, and we take captive every thought to make it obedient to Christ.

2 Corinthians 10:5 NIV

Irony was the weapon used by Kierkegaard to demolish the arguments of his contemporaries who wished to have Christianity conform to current ways of thinking. In the passage quoted above, he ridiculed the dogma of inevitable progress. Technology had by then begun to transform the world. But Kierke-

157

gaard's target was a wider one than technological progress by itself. For he went on to write, "Think of the liberal constitutions, those incomparably perfect discoveries—the pride of the human race—and it arouses longing for an Eastern Despotism as something more fortunate to live under."

Kierkegaard spoke so harshly about liberal constitutions not because he favored authoritarian government but because he foresaw the dangers in them which hardly anyone else at the time imagined. He spoke of what he called *the leveling process*. Today we know that process as mass culture spread through the mass media. What made Kierkegaard apprehensive was his perception that the leveling process meant doing away with all notions of objective right and wrong. It meant the triumph of the amoral will.

The most famous of all liberal constitutions is the one proposed by the American Declaration of Independence of 1776. The declaration made the assertion that "all men are created equal," so that the state must recognize its citizens' rights—"unalienable rights"—to "life, liberty, and the pursuit of happiness." These assertions were "self-evident" truths. (In his first draft of the Declaration, Thomas Jefferson had called them "sacred and undeniable" truths.) Because of the pragmatic outlook of the American tradition and the wisdom of so many of the country's leaders, the united States of America has grown to become the acknowledged leader of the Western world. In the eyes of many—not only in its country of origin—the Declaration of Independence has been regarded as a document second only to Holy Writ. Yet it has sown ideas that are of fateful consequence.

The peace of the earthly city is summed up well in the Declaration: the expectation of its citizens that they will be allowed to live their own lives in their own way, protected by the law and order provided by the state. Yet an unalienable right to this kind of life is something which no actually existing state can guarantee. Any state can only make these rights conditional on circumstances. Clearly, the government of the United States has often limited the rights of its citizens, conscripting them into the armed forces, putting many of them in its prisons, and exacting the death penalty for certain crimes. Life, liberty, and the pursuit of happiness is allowed only to loyal citizens, and to those only sometimes.

The principle of equality is even more limited. Quite apart from the fact that for a long time Americans accepted chattel slavery with a good conscience, equality of wealth was never remotely considered desirable. Yet economic inequalities most nearly touch the everyday life of everyone. No state can ever guarantee anything more than equality before the law. As George Orwell stated in his satire on the communist state, *Animal Farm* (1945), the principle of equality always works out in practice to mean, "all animals are equal, but some animals are more equal than others." The unalienable right to equality can hardly be deduced from creation. The biblical view is that God loves each of his creatures with an equal love. This can hardly be translated into the view that the state must behave as God does. It certainly cannot be translated into the principle that all social groups can demand that the state guarantee their rights unconditionally.

The basic facts are these. The state exists through holding on to power, and so all power belongs to the state. It has all the rights there are; and, in the last resort, its citizens have only duties. The state may grant its citizens certain conditional rights, removing these when its own existence is threatened. A constitution, interpreted through a body of law, inhibits the state from taking arbitrary action. Thus it is a precious protection for all citizens. But any constitution claiming the rights of citizens to be original and unconditional is indulging in rhetoric having no relation to an actually existing situation. It is making a religious affirmation concerning what it considers *sacred*. Or, if all reference to God and the sacred is omitted, it is appealing to an abstract moral principle. That is, it is setting up a particular theory about what constitutes social justice.

In the parable of Jesus about the workers in the vineyard (Matt. 20:1-16), the workers who had worked all day objected to receiving the same wages as those working only a short time.

The principle of equal pay for equal work had been violated. Jesus told his parable to explain how God's kingdom does not recognize special merit, but is a kingdom of grace, one in which the first are last and the last first. In place of abstract principles God puts the concrete gift of all-embracing love. Kierkegaard laughed at the emphasis which his age had begun to lay upon moral principles, seeing this attitude as evidence of an attempt to substitute human ideals for the will of God. He said that if one worked at it, one could elevate into a principle having an extra button on one's coat. The leveling process led logically to the notion that one person's idea of right and wrong was as good as anyone else's idea. Therefore people had only to assert that they regarded something to be a moral principle in order to make that thing right and all other ideas wrong. Christians, on the other hand, regarded right and wrong to lie in the will of God. If they were to have Christian ideas concerning right and wrong, they had to cultivate obedient thinking. Their duty lay in doing God's will and finding their happiness in serving him and their neighbors.

The principle of equality illustrates well how thinking in terms of abstract principles leads people away from considering not only the will of God but also the practical conditions of living on God's earth.

If all have been created equal, then no one should be compelled to serve anyone else. Yet without this kind of service human communities could not survive. Aristotle's rational analysis of society accepted the institution of slavery as a law of nature. Medieval Catholic thinking took over from Aristotle the theory of natural law, and therefore also accepted slavery. In classical culture, slaves often enjoyed more actual freedom than today's urban poor. Abolishing the institution of slavery does not necessarily result in making the citizens of the state more equal. In order to continue to exist, the state has to see that its citizens continue to serve its interests, either through specific legislation directed to force people to work, or else through economic pressure built into the social system. A society of free and equal persons organized politically is a theory that does not work in practice. A Marxist state theoretically should be one in which there is no problem at all over human rights or over economic efficiency. Yet we see how these are precisely the problems that today have brought communist countries to crisis and revolt. Capitalism, based on individuals having freedom to follow their own selfish interests, seems to work better. Yet here too practice lags behind theory. Human rights are in theory recognized and supported by legislation, as are the conditions under which people work. Still, the nexus of unfreedom (to use Ernest Becker's term) pervades the free countries, perpetuating an enormous amount of human misery.

Political organization is possible only when there is a hierarchy of power. This is seen perhaps most clearly in the armed services, the establishment upon which, in the last resort, the power of the state depends. The military chain of command culminating in a supreme commander is the *sine qua non* of this establishment. Consequently, a military dictatorship is rightly regarded as the most despotic form of government—the last resort abolishes all the freedoms won over the years by a tradition in which the power of the state is limited by law and by custom. Yet liberal democracy requires for its existence a bureaucracy of power. Bureaucratic establishments are as fully hierarchical in their structures as are the armed forces. Legislation intended to ensure certain kinds of equality among the citizens of a democratic state, therefore, has to be processed by an establishment itself the very epitome of unequality. The state is saying, in effect, "If you wish to be free and equal, then obey my servants or take the consequences!" George Orwell was right. In the human farm, all animals can be equal only when some animals are more equal than others.

In a technological society, the question of equality is muddied because many differences between people that used to be important now scarcely matter. In traditional societies of an earlier date, agriculture was at the center. Bodily strength was needed for work on the land, and new bodies were required in every new generation. Women's work was to produce children and to assist in the more routine (and often more laborious) manual labor. Men did the organizing and planning as well as those tasks where strength was required, and they were conscripted into the fighting forces. A clear division of labor was the rule. The New Testament says that in Christ there is no distinction between Jew and Greek, slave and free, male and female (Gal. 3:28). There are few distinctions in the technological society either, provided one can fill in forms, run a computer, and drive a car. Technically, every one is free and equal. At the same time, the multiplication of social movements demanding human rights for different segments of the population indicates that inequalities not only persist but are felt to be more and more oppressive.

There is only one way out of the impasse created by the illusion that the modern state exists to legislate perfect equality among all groups of citizens demanding immediate liberation. This is to halt in our efforts to turn state power into the servant of all, which it can never be. The state will always be the servant only of power groups which collectively succeed in imposing their will upon its will. Government of the people, by the people, and for the people is a fine ideal. It is perhaps, as Reinhold Niebuhr would say, an impossible possibility that may inspire us to approximate it. But it is utopian theory and not a practical goal. We need to transfer our energies from trying to make collectivities into the utopias they never can become, and instead concentrate upon building up communities. And the Christian churches are in a unique position to undertake this task.

Social salvation is an impossible combination of words. Society cannot be saved from sin, because society cannot recognize sin, only social evils. The just society is an impossible possibility; but it is not something which the Christian church can take as its mission, because the state is "the beast from the bottomless pit" and the attempt to have Satan cast out our Satan is doomed from the start. The church of Jesus Christ exists on earth to proclaim that here we have no lasting city and we seek one to come—one which *will* come in God's good time. Before that time comes, Christians do not sit with folded hands, knowing that their souls are secure. They are called to active obedience: "Continue to work out your salvation with fear and trembling, for it is God who works in you to will and to act according to his good purpose" (Phil. 2:12-13 NIV).

Fear and Trembling (1843) is Kierkegaard's best-known book, the one in which he explained what it meant to be an individual self before God. The words from St. Paul's letter to the Philippians express how every Christian should feel before acting in the world. Even a seemingly trivial deed of ours may start a train of consequences which could result in desolating the whole world. While anything so drastic is unlikely, acts we perform without fear and trembling may very easily hurt our neighbor against our intention. And we may well imperil our salvation at those times when we most boldly and confidently proclaim that we are fulfilling God's good purposes. At such times, we are likely to be taking God's name in vain as an excuse for pleasing ourselves.

In fear and trembling then, Christians have a duty to their neighbors after they first have sought to be the obedient children of God. Obeying in action goes together with obeying in thought, for action proceeds from the thoughts of our hearts. The New Testament says nothing about our building the kingdom, but it speaks continually about edifying or building up the fellowship of the church through loving deeds. In the church, we are brought to know what life in community means in a much more comprehensive way than we experience it within the community of our own families. In the church, the body of Christ, we are not united through blood ties but through the blood of Jesus Christ shed to save sinners. We learn to love our neighbor, often our unlikable neighbor, because we and this neighbor worship together as forgiven sinners. And Christian neighbors, neighbors because of a common faith, are not simply learning to behave with neighbor-love. In the church they are always learning to think as Christ's disciples, putting both heart and mind at the disposal of their Lord. A somewhat cynical saying is that God gives us our friends in compensation for having forced our relatives upon us. In the church, God calls us to recognize as friends people whom we would never have chosen willingly as friends; people who, were they relatives, we would avoid.

It almost goes without saying, therefore, that the churches begin to act like the church of Jesus Christ when they work at edifying or building up the local congregations, making them into communities rather than loose associations of like-minded people or social clubs. Most churches, indeed, work fairly hard in this direction. They wish the congregations to be more than a collection of people who meet for Sunday services of worship and then forget about one another until the following Sunday. Yet all too often these same churches try to encourage a community spirit through trying to involve their members in good causes which will bring them together for action. There is nothing wrong with that, except that enthusiasm for a common cause and the excitement of working on group projects may have nothing whatsoever to do with obedient service to Christ. The churches become genuinely part of the Church when they earnestly seek to do God's will and not their own, when they seek to obey their Lord rather than conform to what the world around them is ready to call relevant service. And taking this step demands obedient thinking. It means questioning the contemporary world's demands for equality reached by political action. And it means contrasting the world's understanding of liberation with the humble and happy freedom found in Jesus Christ.

The mission of the churches is easy to define. It is simply to preach the gospel and to edify their members, seeking to grow more effective in carrying out these duties—more effective in greater obedience to their Lord. Increase in membership is one sign of effectiveness; yet it is a sign of disobedience when numbers become a preoccupation to the exclusion of concern for the edification of members already there. Edification is a long and painful task as well as a joyful duty. It requires both fear and trembling before God and hard thinking and plain speaking before our neighbors if there is to be loving communication of God's truth.

The churches are not called upon by their Lord to try to

perfect the social order. Their mandate does not include giving orders to the powers-that-be, though on occasion they may be compelled to protest some action of the state that Christians cannot accept in silence because silence for them would mean sinful complicity in intolerable evil. On these occasions, however, all Christians may not be of one mind. The churches must have very good reason for their protests and also firm grounds for thinking that their speaking will have practical results. Mere moral indignation is not Christian love in action.

The churches, all the same, have as part of their teaching mission the obligation to help their members understand the world in which they are living. Being alert to the nature of Babylon and Philistia is part of every Christian's education. Individual Christians have to live in the world, mix in society at many levels, and join different social groups. Christians are found in many political parties as well as in voluntary associations having concerns leading them to take political action. Here is a wide field where obedient thinking is urgent, since the direction of thought taken always determines the practical plans drawn up for implementation. Policies are born out of concepts. When theories are wholly abstract, the odds are that trying to put them into practice may at some time desolate the earth.

One of the most important of the traditional means of edification in the churches has always been Bible study. Because the Bible is so concrete in content, it is the best place to go to prevent our thinking from soaring away from the earth entirely. Yet studying Scripture can bring no results if Christians look there simply for confirmation of ideas that are already in their heads. There are always texts which, taken in isolation, will support or at least seem to support conclusions which the Bible continually rejects. So Christians may end up thinking of a human Jesus who is purely a moral example; of a Christ who has nothing to do essentially with the Word made flesh; of salvation which reads sin as social evil and the communion of saints as an earthly utopia; of the redemption of the world as the culmination of a process turning matter into spirit; and of the living God as the future God. Using the Bible is one thing, and it does not edify. Listening to the Bible is quite another thing. It edifies even when Christians disagree upon details by no means unimportant in themselves.

If the churches use the Bible study to listen obediently to what God is saying, then one thing becomes very plain about the contemporary world. Our world has lost the sense of community and is mourning for what it has lost without necessarily knowing why it mourns. Pursuing happiness in every likely and unlikely place, it finds only frustration in the world-weariness driving it to senseless consumption and the oblivion of narcotics. If God allows those who obey him "a humble but purposeful and really happy freedom of movement," then the Bible will disclose to us where happiness actually lies. The pursuit of happiness in the thinking of our world and in obedient thinking is one last subject to be considered.

18. Earthly Good—Under Heaven: Epilogue to Part Two

*Happy are the people in such a case as ours;
happy the people who have the Lord for their God.*

Psalm 144:15 NEB

Happy those who hunger and thirst for what is right: they shall be satisfied.

Matthew 5:6 JB

We ought to find and love God in what he actually gives us; if it pleases him to allow us to enjoy some overwhelming earthly happiness, we must not try to be more pious than God himself and allow our happiness to be corrupted by presumption and arrogance, and by unbridled religious fantasy which is never satisfied with what God gives. God will see to it that the man who finds him in his earthly happiness and thanks him for it does not lack reminder that earthly things are transient, that it is good for him to attune his heart to what is eternal.

Dietrich Bonhoeffer

Obedient thinking means to cease bowing down before the power of Babylon the Great. It means that certain Christians will no longer run around in the land of the Philistines crying, "What you wish, we wish! Your idols are our idols! Your utopia is our utopia!" When prodigal churches recover respect for their traditions, they will remember how the gospel teaches opposition to the ways of the world for the sake of God's kingdom and, because of that, out of care for the earth.

Care for the earth involves appreciating earthly good wherever it is found, because all good comes from God as his gift to the inhabitants of earth. Everything that is good in our social structures is the sign of God's continued care for us, telling us that he has never left himself with evidence of himself, just as he has shown himself in the bounty of nature (Acts 14:17). Such good reminds us that our Creator intended us to live in communities. Sinfully, we have preferred to live in collectivities where we imagine we shall be able to please ourselves.

The task of building up community instead of collectivity is a complex one and could be the subject of many books. Yet the direction to be taken is clear enough. It would begin with the smallest of communities, the human family. In our day the family is being atomized because of our culture's preoccupation with the triumph of the will. We indulge our children out of guilt, knowing that we are not prepared to give them the one thing they need: security in relationships. When today a parent says to a child, "I love you very much," there is often this unspoken comment: "but not as much as my own inclinations if I happen to find a sexual partner more to my liking than your mother (or father)." Christians should know that faithfulness in marriage is their creaturely duty, since the Creator is faithful in his covenant love.

Jesus wept over the earthly Jerusalem of his day, saying, "Would that even today you knew the things that make for peace!" (Lk. 19:42 RSV). In every age people turn unthinkingly to seek the peace of Babylon, and live to find that peace a desolation. In the same way, they turn to pursue happiness as the world imagines it.

168

In the Declaration of Independence, the pursuit of happiness was conceived in terms of Enlightenment thinking. The American founding fathers probably had a reasonably clear idea in their minds about what they meant when they spoke of this "unalienable right." Their tastes being largely those of English country gentlemen, for them the pursuit of happiness consisted in the good husbandry of their possessions, advancing the public good through charitable works and wise legislation, and following virtue (civilized traditions) under the guidance of a God revealed by reason. It probably never occurred to them that later generations of Americans would think of the good life in very different terms. In a free nation, virtue was bound to flourish more and more!

When it comes to the pursuit of happiness today, the rush towards collectivism shows its other face of irresponsible individualism. Such individualism is the polar opposite of the understanding that the individual stands before God and therefore is called to neighbor-love. The modern individual is simply a unit in the crowd, a consumer of the products of technology, an empty vessel into which the mass media can pour its messages, an expression of the collective will to power and riches. When antisocial, this individual is the terrorist and the drug addict.

Yet God created us as individuals so that we might receive his gift of happiness. In the Old Testament there is never any doubt that our happiness on earth comes from God and is to be received gratefully. "Happy is the people in such a case as ours,"—when we can enjoy the fruits of our labor, live in peace with our neighbor, and obey the God who is righteous and calls us to his righteousness. In the New Testament the lesson is no different, except that now happiness is extended to the world to come. Christians live in expectation of God's kingdom found in a new heaven and a new earth.

Oddly, hardly any of the modern translations of the Bible use the word "happy" when they come to what are traditionally called the Beatitudes of Jesus, preferring the now archaic word "blessed." Yet the Greek for the New Testament uses the ordinary term for happiness in the sense of *to be envied*. Somehow translators seem to be under the impression that Jesus wished people to be happy in a religious way, pursuing some kind of *higher happiness* requiring the special world "blessed." Certainly Jesus taught that happiness was not to be found by following the ways of this world—the lowly and the mourners and the persecuted are not the models of happiness in the world's eyes. Yet, as his parable shows quite clearly, all happy people share the same happiness. The shepherd who finds his lost sheep is happy with the same happiness that is known by those who suffer for the sake of the gospel and the gospel's Lord.

What is wrong with our sinful view of happiness is that we try to pursue it, instead of accepting it as it comes from God. We should hunger and thirst after righteousness. (Here the translation of the verse from Matthew's Gospel, given above, is inadequate; "what is right" suggests a mere moral good, while righteousness in the New Testament always means the quality of God's kingdom). Hungering and thirsting after happiness is self-defeating. Bonhoeffer understood the unity of all happiness, earthly or heavenly. In one of his prison letters he said that all Christians should steep themselves in the Old Testament before they read the New Testament—meaning before they thought themselves competent to interpret the New Testament. Like Karl Barth, Bonhoeffer put a high value upon Ecclesiastes as a book for Christian reading. "For everything there is a season" (Eccl. 3:1 RSV). Bonhoeffer quoted this verse in order to comment that, when the time comes, a Christian will long to "be with the Lord." Before that time arrives, to refuse the earthly joys God puts in our path is arrogance and religious fantasy.

A Christian such as Bonhoeffer, who spoke of earthly happiness from a prison cell at a time when he realized he might never find freedom except in death, is not to be lightly disregarded. So too, Christians who seek to find ways our present political, social, and cultural life may be improved to bring more happiness on earth are doing the Lord's work and praying "Thy kingdom come." But everything depends upon our seeing earthly good in the light of heavenly righteousness.

Reinhold Niebuhr argued that utopian dreams are the

reverse of Christian realism. The corridors of power can never lead to God's righteous kingdom. At best, political and social organizations may better the human condition a little; yet freedom gained in one place is at the expense of freedom lost in another. To estimate the balance between gain and loss taxes our limited wisdom. But unrealistic expectations are the worst of follies.

Having followed the ways of Babylon for so long, the churches may find the road back to the service of Jerusalem a hard one. Yet Christians have the assurance that God never abandons his children, however rebellious they prove, however much they refuse to be his people. Christ promised that the powers of death should not prevail against his Church. Although the Lord of the Dance of Death masquerading as the Lord of Life has gained entry into the churches, his reign is—as it must always be—insecure. Martin Luther's great hymn is still sung in the churches:

> And let the prince of ill,
> Look grim as e'er he will,
> He harms us not a whit;
> For why, his doom is writ;
> A word shall quickly slay him.

That word is the Word made flesh. Those who trust in their Incarnate Lord do not fear the powers of the present or of the future. Our God remains Lord of the earth, and in his will is our peace. The Father who sent his Son for our salvation calls us to happiness here and hereafter.

When the prodigal churches return home, there will be rejoicing in heaven. On the human level, there will be the hope for earthly good.